TOOTSIETOYS
World's First Diecast Models

James Wieland

Edward Force

Photographs by Thomas Budney of Bantam, Connecticut

Motorbooks International
Publishers & Wholesalers Inc.
Osceola, Wisconsin 54020, USA

© 1980 by James Wieland and Edward Force
ISBN: 0-87938-065-9
Library of Congress Number: 79-22376

Motorbooks International is a certified trademark, registered with
the United States Patent Office.

Printed and bound in the United States of America.

Book and cover design by William F. Kosfeld.

10   9   8   7   6   5   4   3

Library of Congress Cataloging in Publication Data

Wieland, James, 1946-
   Tootsietoys, world's first diecast models.

   1.   Die-cast toys.   2.   Automobiles—Models.
I.   Force, Edward, 1938-   joint author.   II.   Title.
TS2301.T7W47   688.7'28   79-22376
ISBN 0-87938-065-9 pbk.

Contents

Introduction

Tootsietoys! There is a magic in the name for those of us who played with them in childhood, whether we see them now as treasured collectors' items or as fond memories of joyful younger days. If our memories—and our lives—go back far enough, we can recall a glowing golden day when a nickel or a dime bought us a toy that was more than just another plaything. It was a car, a truck, a train or plane in metal, a miniature replica of a real vehicle from the big, fascinating world around us. Real—that was what made the difference; for with imagination the miniature grew to full size and so did we, and the sandbox or the railroad platform became the real world. Engines roared, wheels turned, tires squealed—until our mothers called us to supper and we became children again, and no longer drivers, pilots, engineers, things we couldn't be until we grew up—and growing up took a long time. We were impatient then, impatient for the time to come when imagination would become reality. Of course, when we grew up the real world didn't always turn out to be what we had imagined, and we looked back, and still do, with bittersweet nostalgia for the days when we were young and skies were blue. Our spouses may sigh that we're still kids at heart, but we know we've changed, and in more than mere height and weight. The world around us has changed, and so have Tootsietoys. Perhaps that's why we're kids at heart: because things have changed, because the sky is less blue and life less sweet. All the more reason to return in our dreams to the golden days when we held in our hands a link between a child's imagination and a fascinating real world: a Tootsietoy!

The story of the diecast motor vehicles that came to be known as Tootsietoys goes back to 1910. The history of their manufacturers, though, began in the nineteenth century, and will serve as a brief introduction to our description of the models themselves. It must be noted that, though the firm is still in existence and still produces toy vehicles, the collector's interest is chiefly in the Tootsietoys produced before World War II; thus the greater portion of our text will concern the prewar models. Their story has been told in print before, but not always with complete accuracy, and controversy has arisen. We are particularly indebted to C.B.C. Lee's series of articles that first appeared in the British *Model Cars* magazine in 1971, and to Louis H. Hertz's *The Complete Book of Building and Collecting Model Automobiles*, for the documented historical facts that we shall summarize briefly here.

The story begins in 1876, when Charles O. Dowst of Chicago founded the firm of Dowst and Company to publish a trade paper, the *National Laundry Journal*. Soon the firm began to manufacture various laundry supplies as well. At the Columbian Exposition held in Chicago in 1893, Mr. Dowst encountered a new machine known then as the Line-o-Type. He and his brother Samuel, who had joined the firm (which became the Dowst Brothers Company), realized that such a machine could cast not only lines of type but collar buttons and other laundry accessories too. The casting machine soon led them into new fields of business: small toys, bracelet charms, prizes for Cracker Jacks, and other novelties. By 1899 the firm was listed as a manufacturer of confectioners' supplies; by 1904 its products were described as metal novelties. The transition from the laundry, via the candy store, to the toyshop was in progress.

In 1906 a second-generation Dowst joined the firm in the person of Theodore Samuel Dowst, bookkeeper. Ted Dowst remained with the firm until 1945, when he retired as its president. His career was one of innovation and progress in the designing, assembling and selling of toys. The firm took its first major step in this direction in 1910 and 1911, when its first miniature vehicles were produced. Though the first car, the well-known Limousine of 1911, represented a generic car of the era rather than any specific make, the firm's second miniature car, issued in 1914, was a model of the Model T Ford. From then on, most Tootsietoys were more or less faithful reproductions of real vehicles, though their parentage was not always acknowledged. In time, though, manufacturers of real vehicles learned that models of their products were a good form of advertising, and in later years several firms subsidized the making of Tootsietoy models of their cars and trucks.

Until at least 1920 the few miniature vehicles made by the firm were marketed, along with its other toys and novelties, under the name of Dowst. In the next few years the name of Tootsietoy (sometimes printed or cast into the toys as two words) made its appearance on Dowst products. The process of registering the trade name was completed in 1924, and slowly but surely it was seen on more and more of the firm's toys. As late as 1930, though, some of the firm's products still did not physically bear the name of Tootsietoy.

Regardless of these omissions, the name was well established by then. It has remained in use to this day despite changes in the firm's ownership and corporate structure. In 1926 the firm was sold by the Dowsts to Nathan Shure, who merged it with his Cosmo toy and novelty firm but retained the name of Dowst Manufacturing Company and the talents of Ted Dowst. The change of ownership in 1926 has been misinterpreted by at least one chronicler, who assumed that the firm as a whole was founded, and the first Tootsietoys produced, in 1926!

Since that date the firm's history has been one of expansion and progress. No major changes in the corporate structure have taken place other than the purchase of the Strombecker Corporation in 1964. The name of the acquired firm became that of the company as a whole, but the Tootsietoy trade name was retained and is still in use. Several important innovations in the techniques and materials of manufacturing took place over the years and have made their mark on the toy industry. Casting procedures became more sophisticated, allowing more precisely detailed models. The Model T Ford of 1914 had introduced the use of a separate casting comprising windshield, dashboard, steering column and wheel; a separate radiator grille casting was first used on the Model A Ford in 1928. The 1933 Graham series introduced three-piece miniature car construction (separate body, chassis and radiator grille castings), while the LaSalles of 1935 included a fourth casting for the rear bumper.

In 1933 more progress in the toy industry was made than the three-piece construction that was soon adopted by such giants as Dinky Toys and Märklin. In this year numerous Tootsietoys appeared with separate diecast wheel hubs and rubber tires, replacing the all-metal wheels in which hub and tire were represented by a single metal casting. Even if they were white, the rubber tires gave Tootsietoys a more realistic appearance than before. More important was the use of Zamak, a zinc alloy, in place of the softer, heavier lead alloy used until then. The use of Zamak made for lighter, sturdier castings.

The coming of war led not only to the manufacture of models of military vehicles, but also, as supplies of materials grew short, to the use of such substitutes as wood for wheels. On June 30, 1942, all toy production had to cease for the duration of the war. It was resumed late in 1945 and has continued ever since, but with a difference in the nature of the toys. It is said that in 1935 Ted Dowst declared, "We make toys for doodling, not models for collecting." Since then most of the firm's toy vehicles have been designed as inexpensive toys rather than detailed scale models. The firm's commercial success has continued, but the interest of collectors has all but disappeared. With the deletion of older models and production of new ones after the war, the effect of the 'doodling' policy made itself felt much more strongly than in the few years just before it, and the wartime cessation of production forms an effective division between the collectors' items of the good old days and the toys of more modern times.

We would welcome comments, corrections and additions to this book.

James Wieland
E2 Tapping Reeve
Litchfield, Connecticut 06759

Dr. Edward Force
42 Warham Street
Windsor, Connecticut 06095

Prewar

The Dowst firm produced its first miniature vehicles in 1910. There were actually three versions of the aeroplane (the spelling used until World War II) with which Louis Bleriot made the first flight over the English Channel on July 25, 1909. One was of watch-charm size; the second (no. 4491) was about 25 mm long; and the largest (no. 4482) was 67 mm long with a wingspan of 84 mm. To the modern observer it does not look much like an airplane, but aircraft were primitive in those days. The model consists of an uncovered fuselage frame, simple wings and stabilizers, a big propeller and three spoked-metal wheels. Except for the added propeller and wheels, it is a single casting. The model remained in production for at least fifteen years, attesting to strong public interest in aircraft.

A year later, in 1911, the firm's first miniature car was produced, the no. 4258 Limousine. A period piece to modern eyes, it portrays a generic car-type of its time—a high, narrow, closed car, rather than a specific make of car. The single casting is 47 mm long, has detailed doors, windows, a long, louvered hood and runs on spoked metal wheels. Even non-collectors find its nostalgic atmosphere irresistible.

Unlike the Limousine, the firm's second car model represents a real vehicle, the Model T Ford. At first this miniature, no. 4570, was advertised merely as an 'Automobile' and compared to "the well known Flivver," which identified it to the public as a Ford. By 1925 it was listed in the firm's sales literature by its true name. An open touring car, 77 mm long, it is composed of a main body casting plus a separate windshield/dashboard/steering-wheel casting crimped into a slot in the body. The car runs on four cast-metal wheels, originally a sturdy spoked design and later solid discs representing the clincher-type Disteel wheels in vogue at the time. These became the prevailing type of Tootsietoy wheels until 1933, when rubber tires were introduced. Casting details of the Model T Ford include four doors, hood louvers, seat-cushion and floorboard patterns and a folded top; but its grille, like that of the Limousine, is completely featureless. The model remained in production until 1926 and marked a milestone in toy production, for it was, as far as we know, the first diecast miniature of a real car made in America—and what better car to be so honored than the one whose production revolutionized industry all over the world?

Another Ford model appeared in 1916, this time an open Model T pickup truck, no. 4610, called simply Truck even after the tourer's ancestry had been acknowledged. The front half of the 77 mm casting is much like the Model T tourer; it has no doors, but the seat and floorboard patterns are the same, and the same windshield casting is fitted. The rear half consists of a simple open-box body. The model remained in production until 1932, outlasting the tourer by six years because of its use in several boxed sets of Tootsietoys.

By the end of its first decade of miniature vehicle production the firm had produced only these few models. It was a slow beginning, but it gave at least a hint of the progress that was to come, though it came slowly at first. The Dowst sales catalogue for 1921 shows no new models. The Model T tourer is still called Automobile. The Truck is simply the "companion piece to our famous no. 4570 Automobile," the Limousine is "undoubtedly one of the best selling small toys ever put on the market," and the Aeroplane is still "a sure sale to any boy who sees it."

The 1921 catalogue also shows a wide variety of other diecast items, including housewares, whistles, animals on wheels, tops, a telephone, a water pistol, a Liberty Bell, an old-fashioned passenger train and two other vehicles. These last three deserve mention as curiosities if nothing else. One vehicle purports to be "a faithful, clever reproduction" of Robert Fulton's steamboat, the *Clermont*. One wonders what the scoffers who called that pioneering vessel 'Fulton's Folly' would have called this toy. Despite its turning paddle wheel, tall

NO. 4482 BLERIOT AEROPLANE, ISSUED IN 1910. 67 MM LONG; THERE WAS ALSO A SMALLER VERSION AVAILABLE (NO. 4491).

NO. 4528 LIMOUSINE, ISSUED IN 1911. THIS WAS THE FIRST CAR PRODUCED BY THE FIRM. 47 MM LONG.

NO. 4570 AUTOMOBILE, ISSUED IN 1914. ALSO CALLED FLIVVER IN ADVERTISING AFTER 1925. REPRESENTS A 1914 MODEL T FORD. 1/48 SCALE, 77 MM.

NO. 4610 TRUCK, A 1914 MODEL T FORD PICKUP, WAS ISSUED IN 1916. 1/48 SCALE, 77 MM.

NO. 4629 SEDAN, KNOWN AS 1921 YELLOW CAB, WAS ISSUED IN 1923. 1/48 SCALE, 72 MM.

smokestack and silly representation of a walking-beam engine—not to mention the name cast on its bow—no. 4465 is far from being a scale model of the *Clermont* or any other real steamboat. It is an amusing little toy, and it has a certain charm. So does its one-nanny-power companion, the no. 4400 Folding Go-Cart. This item appears to consist of two main castings that fold where a pin joins them; it runs on four spoked-metal wheels. It is, of course, not a motor vehicle, but only a pedant could resist mentioning it.

Both of these items may have been introduced well before 1921, and the same applies to the no. 4397 Train. It consists of four pieces: a nineteenth century locomotive with massive cowcatcher, big headlight, tall smokestack, oversize bell and general air of antiquity; a similarly old-fashioned tender that seems to have number 899 cast into its sides; and two dolefully ornate coaches. Like the 4-4-0 locomotive, the other three pieces appear to have two sets of four wheels apiece, but these may be parts of the castings covering simpler and less numerous actual wheels. The whole train is "finished in silver plate," which must make it look all the more like a specter from the past. Unlike the Clermont and the Go-Cart, this train went out of production before 1925.

Only in 1923 was another model car added to the line that was just beginning to bear the Tootsietoy name. Collectors usually call no. 4629 the 'Yellow Cab,' but it was advertised simply as Sedan. It was the first Tootsietoy to have a detailed radiator grille, but otherwise it is a bit on the dull side, with a high, boxy body 72 mm long. Fortunately it is a wider and thus more stable model than the Fords or the Limousine. Its details, including four doors, large hood louvers, cast-in rear spare wheel and the aforementioned radiator grille, are fairly good. The car runs on four Disteel wheels, which had replaced the earlier spoked-type by this time. Its city-bred air, plus the fact that it was often painted yellow (though it also appeared in the other customary Tootsietoy colors of red, blue and green) must have inspired its unofficial name. It was popular enough to stay in production through 1933, and to be copied by at least five other toy makers, in England and France as well as America.

Its popularity was at least equaled by "a 'sure fire' seller" introduced in 1924: the no. 4636 Coupe. Though not identified as such, it resembles a Series 50 Buick of the time. The single casting is 76 mm long and includes a detailed grille shaped rather like an old-fashioned tombstone with rounded head and square shoulders, a trunk or rumble-seat lid with seven longitudinal stripes, and two cast-in side spare wheels represented by patterns of concentric circles. Despite its angular styling, the Coupe looks more modern and sporty than any Tootsietoy that preceded it. Like the Sedan, it remained in production through 1933 and inspired numerous diecast and slushmold copies.

The long production runs of these models have made them fairly common among early Tootsietoys. But 1924 also brought a series of Delivery Vans whose regular members, with one exception, are quite rare, and whose special issues are among the rarest of all Tootsietoys. They bear some resemblance to Federal trucks and are often so called by collectors, but the Dowst firm, as usual at that time, did not identify them as to make.

The vans made for general retail sale included six versions with different names cast on their sides, but all numbered 4630: Grocery (issued until 1929), Bakery (dropped before 1929), Market (also dropped early), Laundry (likewise), Milk (which lasted until 1933) and Florist (another early deletion). Authorities agree that the Milk Van is most common and the Florist Van rarest, with the other four not as rare as the Florist but much more so than the Milk Van. Mr. Hertz feels that a mother seeking a toy to take home to her child would probably have chosen the Milk Van in preference to the other five, and that children would have been least likely to relate to the Florist Van.

The design of the vans combines sturdiness with a degree of stateliness which makes them something more than mere workhorses. The grille has a simpler tombstone shape than that of the Coupe, but behind it the hood flares out at each side to form ninety-degree angles with its vertical panels. The styling around the doors adds a touch of class, as do the elliptical

NO. 4636 COUPE, REP-
RESENTS 1924 BUICK SERIES
50 COUPE, ISSUED IN 1924.
1/48 SCALE, 76 MM.

NO. 4630 DELIVERY VANS:
LAUNDRY AND GROCERY.
STANDARD ISSUES FROM
THE 1924 DELIVERY VANS
SERIES, REPRESENTATIVE
OF 1924 FEDERAL VANS. 1/48
SCALE, 75 MM.

NO. 4630 DELIVERY VANS:
MILK AND BAKERY.

NO. 4630 DELIVERY VANS:
FLORIST AND MARKET.

NO. 4630 DELIVERY VANS
(SPECIAL ISSUES): WATT &
SHAND; ADAM, MELDRUM &
ANDERSON CO. MADE IN
1924, SPECIAL ISSUES OF
THE DELIVERY VANS SERIES
ARE AMONG THE RAREST
TOOTSIETOYS.

side and rear windows. The vans are single castings, 75 mm long, running on Disteel wheels.

The story of the Delivery Vans does not stop here, for a number of special issues were made. With one exception they were produced for, and bore the names of, department stores or toyshops that, presumably, sold large quantities of Tootsietoys. Most of the stores were located in the Northeast, and Mr. Lee, who has written two articles on these special vans, observes that all were within reach, by train, of Dowst's New York office chief, Rollo Ballenger, who personally arranged for their production. The one exception, totally unlike the others in origin, is lettered 'U.S. Mail' and was found in California about 1969 by collector B. J. Donnelly. Appropriately painted a light gold, it may well be the most valuable single Tootsietoy in existence.

Mr. Lee's research has authenticated the following store vans:

Adam, Meldrum & Anderson (Buffalo, N.Y.): dark red.
L. Bamberger & Co. (Newark, N.J.): dark green.
Boggs & Buhl (Philadelphia, Pa.): blue.
Hochschild, Kohn & Co. (Baltimore, Md.): black and yellow, with decals instead of cast-in lettering.
Jermyn Brothers Toys (Scranton, Pa.): light and dark yellow, blue, red.
J. C. Penney Department Stores (New York, N.Y.): light yellow.
Pomeroy's (Harrisburg, Pa.): green, perhaps more than one shade.
Strawbridge & Clothier (Philadelphia, Pa.): blue.
Watt & Shand (Lancaster, Pa.): gray.

Also rumored to exist but not verified are J. N. Adams & Co., Alling Rubber Co. Toys, Baker's Chocolate, Bon Marche (a department store in Seattle, hardly within a day's train ride of Mr. Ballenger's office), Hengerer's, Jordan Marsh & Co., R. H. Macy, and Smith & Welton versions. One would think that if stores the size of Macy's and Jordan Marsh had had such vans made, some would have survived to this day, so we must draw a big question mark over these unconfirmed names, a few of which may possibly be versions of the later 'Camelback' Van. The mystery helps to make the year of 1924, in which the Tootsietoy name was registered, a truly memorable one.

So too was 1925. The Tootsietoys in production were offered to dealers in the well-known (and recently reprinted) Catalogue 46, which called them "the 'All-the-Time' Line," assuring retailers that "a tremendous demand for small, inexpensive toys and novelties" did not exist only at Christmas: "Dowst toys are good for all year round selling. The constant flow of orders throughout ALL MONTHS OF THE YEAR proves that." A number of items were added to the Tootsietoy line, with the observation that "we are cataloguing only those numbers that we know for certainty are live numbers."

Among the live numbers are ten pages of doll houses and furniture for them; a page and a half of small items including the Clermont, the Statue of Liberty, five candelabras and a more mundane candleholder, three whistles, a water pistol, a telephone, the Folding Go-Cart, and three animals (a horse, a dog and a lion) on wheels; and ten and a half pages of miniature vehicles. The latter includes the two Model T Fords, the Coupe and Sedan, the Limousine and Aeroplane, the Delivery Vans, and several new issues, both individual models and sets.

The one new car of 1925 is the no. 4641 Touring Car, which may have been patterned after the Buicks of the time. "The seats and upholstery are in a contrasting color to the body carrying out our new three color scheme," it was stated, but this never happened, for the plan to equip the model with a separate interior casting, presumably held in place by the axles, was given up. The model appeared as a 78 mm single casting of body and integral 'one-man-top' with the usual details, even including door handles. It was one of the best-proportioned and handsomest of the early Tootsietoys and, like the Sedan and Coupe, it was widely copied by other manufacturers. Like them, too, it remained in production through 1933.

NO. 4630 DELIVERY VANS
(SPECIAL ISSUES): BAM-
BERGER; POMEROY'S.

NO. 4630 DELIVERY VANS
(SPECIAL ISSUES): U.S. MAIL;
HOCHSCHILD, KOHN & CO.
THE U.S. MAIL VAN MAY BE
THE MOST VALUABLE
TOOTSIETOY IN EXISTENCE.

NO. 4630 DELIVERY VANS
(SPECIAL ISSUES): STRAW-
BRIDGE & CLOTHIER;
BOGGS & BUHL.

NO. 4630 DELIVERY VANS
(SPECIAL ISSUES): J.C.
PENNEY; JERMYN TOYS.

NO. 4641 TOURING CAR,
ISSUED IN 1925. REP-
RESENTS A 1924 BUICK
TOURING CAR. 1/48 SCALE,
78 MM.

13

Three trucks issued in 1925 were first called 'Mac' though their real name was obviously one letter longer. The no. 4638 Stake Truck, 4639 Coal Truck and 4640 Tank Truck all used the same chassis-cab casting, that of the roofed but not fully enclosed Mack Bulldog truck, with considerable detail, but lacking several features not added until 1928: the 'M' monogram on the nose of the hood, door handles and hinges, and drive chains to the rear axle. The three body castings attach to the flat rear chassis by two rivets, forming a complete model 82 mm long. The rear body of the Stake Truck is formed of horizontal and vertical bars, that of the Coal Truck is hopper-shaped (and does not actually dump), and that of the Tank Truck includes two filler caps atop the tank. These realistic truck models were very popular, and additional Mack types were added in the next few years. The first three types, revised in 1928, were produced through 1933.

From 1925 to 1931 the no. 170 Interchangeable Truck Set could be had; its box held one Mack chassis and all three bodies, their rivets unflattened so that any body could be put on and taken off the chassis. Also available was the no. 10 Auto and Garage Set of four cars and a folding cardboard garage that looks suspiciously like a barn. The four cars were listed as a Sedan, Truck, Roadster (presumably the Model T tourer) and Touring Car, but the picture shows two Model T flivvers and no. 1925 Touring Car.

The most remarkable item in Catalogue 46 is The World Flyers, "a very amusing and entertaining toy that attracts attention wherever displayed." Its rounded base holds a spiral shaft upon which runs a four-armed attachment to whose arms four Bleriot Aeroplanes are hooked. "The mechanism is so simple that any child can operate it—just pull the flyers to the top and they do the rest—revolve and descend." The planes were cast with loops to which wires from the horizontal arms were attached, and they whirled around as the attachment slid down the spiral shaft. This intriguing toy bore no. 160; its exact life span is not known.

The other vehicles shown are trains, both passenger and freight. All are pulled by the no. 4620 Locomotive, much more modern than its predecessor. The casting portrays a 2-6-0 engine, but only the first and last pairs of drive wheels are the real thing, the other being cast-in dummies. A loop at the rear holds the hitch of the no. 4621 Tender, which has number 221 cast into each side and, like the other cars, runs on spoked metal wheels considerably smaller than those of the locomotive.

Two cars were offered: no. 4623 Pullman Coach and no. 4624 Gondola Car. The Coach looks a bit dated now, though not as much as the earlier one. Each side has a door at each end with steps below, an oval window beside the door, plus seven large windows, and the roof has a raised central panel. The Gondola has an open body with exterior details including 'D.B. & Co.' lettering. Each car, like the Tender, has a hitching loop at one end and a hook at the other.

These four pieces were available separately and also used in several boxed sets. The simpler versions were the no. 4626 Passenger Train Set, which consisted of Engine, Tender and Coach; and the no. 4627 Freight Train Set of Engine, Tender and Gondola. The no. 11 Train and Station Set included a cardboard depot, Engine, Tender and three Coaches.

The 1926 supplement to Catalogue 46 offered three new models. The no. 4650 Biplane, though much more modern than the Bleriot, still looks slightly unreal. The yellow fuselage, 80 mm long, has an open cockpit but is otherwise enclosed, and a turning propeller is attached at the front. The short, wide red wings are a separate casting 58 mm long. The Biplane stands on two cast-metal wheels and its tail skid.

The no. 4651 Safety Coach is a fairly good model of a Fageol bus of the time. Its single casting, 90 mm long, is well detailed and includes six windows on each side, a grille with rounded top, and the usual hood and body lines. It was painted one of the four usual colors and equipped with the usual Disteel wheels. It had been superseded by a newer bus model before its withdrawal at the end of 1933.

Also shown in the 1926 supplement, though some authorities believe that it, like the

NO. 4638 STAKE TRUCK. LIKE THE NO. 4639 COAL AND NO. 4640 TANK TRUCKS, WAS CALLED A 'MAC' AT FIRST, BUT WAS MODELED AFTER THE 1921 MACK AC. ISSUED IN 1925, 1/72 SCALE, 82 MM.

NO. 4639 COAL TRUCK, ISSUED IN 1925. LENGTH 82 MM, SCALE 1/72.

NO. 4640 TANK TRUCK, ISSUED IN 1925. LENGTH 82 MM, SCALE 1/72.

NO. 4626 PASSENGER TRAIN SET, ISSUED ABOUT 1925.

NO. 4627 FREIGHT TRAIN SET, ISSUED ABOUT 1925.

Safety Coach, was not issued until 1927, was the no. 23 Tootsietoy Racer. The firm does not seem to have given this model a four-digit number; presumably the racing number cast into its grille was felt to be sufficient. Mr. Hertz believes the number was chosen because of the 'Twenty-three—Skiddoo' slang expression of the time. Unfortunately the Racer was not similarly jazzy, comparing unfavorably with the bulbous Frontenacs and Monroes of 1920 to say nothing of the sleek Millers and Duesenbergs of the mid-twenties. The open cockpit of the Racer held a cast-metal driver whose square rivet fit into a hole in his seat. The driver often came loose, causing a small controversy among hobbyists as to whether the model was at first issued without a driver. The 74 mm car was painted one of the usual four colors, with a tan driver, and ran on disc wheels of a simpler pattern than the Disteel type. In 1933 these wheels, which were also used on a few other models, were replaced by rubber tires on metal hubs; at the end of that year the Racer was withdrawn from production.

The Tootsietoy firm, taken over in 1926 by Nathan Shure but retaining the talents of Ted Dowst, showed a vigorous reaction to the influx of new capital and new thinking. The variety of models increased, and so did the complexity of their casting and assembly, which made for greater play value and increased sales to offset the greater cost of production. Two models issued in 1927 are good examples of this progress.

They are the no. 4652 Hook and Ladder Truck and the no. 4653 Water Tower, a pair of fire trucks that must have won the hearts of millions of small and not-so-small boys. Collectors sometimes call them Fageol or American-LaFrance trucks, but the firm did not identify them as to make. The Hook and Ladder Truck was advertised as being in "four color effect." It consists of separate chassis and body castings painted red and blue (not necessarily respectively, as both combinations exist), plus gold ladders and either Disteel or plain disc (as on the Racer) wheels usually painted gold, leaving one to wonder what became of the fourth color.

The chassis casting used on both fire trucks includes grille, hood, fenders, running boards and axle holes. The body casting hooks under the dashboard, and the rear axle passes through both castings to complete the job of holding them together. One ladder hangs on a rack on each side of the truck; the third lies atop the body, held in place by raised pins. Two pins on the rear running board provide a mount for one of the interlocking ladders. The length of the truck, complete with its ladders, is 105 mm.

The 91 mm Water Tower uses the same chassis, plus a rear body with two tabs to which the raising tower (a separate casting) is attached. It was correctly advertised as being in three colors: the chassis is red, the body and tower both yellow, and the Disteel or plain disc wheels gold. In 1933, just before the two fire trucks were withdrawn, they appeared with rubber tires on metal hubs.

A boxed Fire Department Set, no. 185, offered a single fire truck chassis, a rear axle that must have been uncrimped, and the two bodies. It apparently did not sell as well as the individual trucks, which is quite understandable, for what child wants two fire trucks with only one chassis? It was withdrawn in 1931.

Another 1927 issue, no. 4654, is a rugged two-piece Farm Tractor, 76 mm long, resembling a Huber Star tractor of the time. It was produced through 1932 and, once a towing loop was added, was used in numerous sets. A military version was also produced for set use. The body casting includes the engine hood, fuel tank, driver, seat and steering wheel. The hood sides are cut away to expose the detailed engine block, which is part of the chassis casting. The body hooks into the chassis at the front, while the rear axle pierces both castings. The two pieces were painted different colors, the chassis being black and the body red, orange or tan. A third color, usually red or tan, was used on the four cast-metal wheels. All four wheels have six spokes; the front ones are smaller than the rear pair. The original version without a towing loop is not significantly rarer than the revised type; perhaps both were produced simultaneously for a time.

NO. 4675 WINGS SEAPLANE, ISSUED IN 1929. LENGTH IS 96 MM, WINGSPAN IS ALSO 96 MM.

NO. 4651 SAFETY COACH, MODEL OF A 1926 FAGEOL BUS, ISSUED ABOUT 1927. IT IS 90 MM AND 1/72 SCALE.

NO. 23 RACER, ISSUED ABOUT 1927. 74 MM LONG.

NO. 4652 HOOK AND LAD-DER TRUCK, ISSUED IN 1927. REPRESENTS A 1926 LA FRANCE FIRE ENGINE. 1/72 SCALE, 105 MM.

NO. 4653 WATER TOWER, ISSUED IN 1927. ANOTHER TYPE OF 1926 LA FRANCE FIRE ENGINE. 1/72 SCALE, 91 MM.

17

The big event of 1927 was the production of the General Motors series of (eventually) thirty different chassis-body combinations. Only twenty-four of these possibilities existed through 1932, for only four of the five chassis types were then made: the Buick, Cadillac, Chevrolet and Oldsmobile. The four are distinguished chiefly by the names cast diagonally across their radiator grilles. The Buick name, the only one in script rather than block capitals, is superimposed on a tombstone-shaped grille of diagonal gridwork. The Cadillac grille is slightly rounded at the corners, wider at the bottom than at the top, and made of vertical lines. The Chevrolet grille is roughly the same shape but smaller, with an emblem breaking the line of its top, and the nameless grille issued in 1933 is much like it in form. The Oldsmobile grille is similar, too, but has a straight top-line and widens more as its sides descend; it too is composed of vertical lines but lacks the separate lower panel of finer, closer lines found on the Cadillac and Chevrolet. The Buick hood flows out to meet its side panels at almost a right angle, while the other hoods are rounded at the sides. The Cadillac hood is longer than the others, but its chassis as a whole is no longer. Otherwise the chassis are much the same, including fenders, running boards, and axle holes.

The six body castings project under the rear edge of the hood and have tabs through which the rear axle passes. To the 60- number of the Buick, 61- of the Cadillac, 62- of the Chevrolet and 63- of the Oldsmobile were added the pairs of digits denoting the body type, forming the usual four-figure numbers for the first twenty-four possible combinations. The -01 number designates an open roadster with seat and folded top, open rumble seat, spare wheel cover (also found on the other four car bodies), and a separate windshield/dashboard/steering-wheel casting rather like those of the Model T Fords. The -02 Coupe has a boxy body with windows, tonneau irons, and the usual spare wheel at the rear. The -03 Brougham and -04 Sedan have closed four-door bodies very similar except that the rearmost window on each side of the Brougham is small and oval, while that of the Sedan is larger and rectangular. The -05 Touring Car, much like the 1925 Tourer, has a raised top resting at the front on two very fragile posts. The final body type is the -06 Delivery Truck, a long screen-side van with an elliptical window in each of its two rear doors. Of the six body types, it alone has no spare wheel, as the rear doors leave no room for it.

It is not known whether all twenty-four body/chassis combinations were actually issued, but since any body fits on any chassis, it is easy to uncrimp the rear axle, remove it, and switch bodies on chassis to make any combination. More Buick chassis were made, and more Coupe and Roadster bodies, than any other. The Touring Car body seems to be rarest, perhaps because of its fragility. The Roadster windshield also broke easily, and though the Roadster is by no means rare, it is very hard to find with an intact original windshield.

Numerous colors were used on the G.M. models, including red, yellow, tan, green, blue, gray, and black, the last two being used only on chassis. All models were issued with contrasting body and chassis colors with the exception of an army staff car in solid tan. Gold or black Disteel wheels were used.

In 1933, just before the whole series was withdrawn, a fifth chassis type was introduced, much like the Chevrolet in its details but with no name on its grille. It was never given a catalogue number, and one wonders why it was made. Because of its short life span it is much rarer than the other chassis. There have been rumors of other chassis, notably an Oakland, as this name appears in the 1928 Tootsietoy catalogue, but this is thought to be a printer's error, as General Motors was phasing the Oakland out and the Pontiac in at that time. We can, then, regard the total of five chassis and six bodies as final.

Scarcely had the G.M. series been produced when the firm prepared another pleasant surprise, advertising it early in 1928 as "The Big Secret of 1927 EXPOSED!" It was the no. 4655 Model A Ford Coupe, the result of close cooperation between Dowst and Ford. This 65 mm model was, if anything, better than any previous Tootsietoy. The details and proportions are unusually precise, and the realistic look of the model is heightened by the use of

NO. 4654 FARM TRACTOR, IS-
SUED IN 1927. PATTERNED
AFTER A 1926 HUBER STAR,
76 MM LONG AND 1/48
SCALE.

EXAMPLES FROM THE 1926
GM SERIES, ISSUED IN 1927:
CADILLAC SEDAN, OLDS-
MOBILE BROUGHAM, BUICK
SEDAN, NO-NAME SEDAN
(SOMETIMES CALLED OAK-
LAND, WAS ISSUED LATER,
IN 1933) AND CHEVROLET
ROADSTER.

NO. 6003 BUICK BROUGHAM.
ONE OF SEVERAL BUICKS IS-
SUED IN 1927 REPRESENT-
ING MODELS FROM THE 1926
BUICK SERIES 50. 1/43
SCALE.

NO. 6102 CADILLAC COUPE.
ONE OF SEVERAL CADIL-
LACS ISSUED IN 1927 REP-
RESENTING MODELS OF THE
1926 CADILLAC STANDARD
V-8. 1/43 SCALE.

NO. 6104 CADILLAC SEDAN,
ISSUED IN 1927. 1/43 SCALE.

five diecast pieces in addition to the body casting. Four are solid metal wheels with raised lines to simulate the spokes of real Ford wheels. The fifth, another of the firm's innovations, consists of radiator shell, grille and headlights. A rivet on its back fits through a hole in a panel of the body casting to hold this piece in place. The use of the separate radiator casting made the model look more real and allowed the body to be painted while the radiator remained in a natural-looking metallic color.

Naturally the Model A Coupe was a popular model, and it is not surprising that it was joined by a Sedan the next year and a Van later. The Coupe, like so many other Tootsietoys, was produced until 1933, and might have lasted longer if the real Model A had not been replaced by newer Fords, just as it had superseded the immortal Model T.

Though the flivver had been withdrawn, the Ford Truck was still in use. It was included in two agricultural sets current around 1928, and survived with them until 1932. One was no. 5010 Farm Set, which included the Ford Truck, the Farm Tractor (with towing loop), and a two-wheeled box trailer, a 67 mm single casting with good interior and exterior detail, a long tongue with a hook for attachment to the Tractor, and two six-spoked metal wheels like the Tractor's rear pair. The trailer and its wheels were painted the same colors as the body and wheels of the Tractor in the set.

In the companion Farm Set, no. 7003, the Ford Truck and Farm Tractor were joined by a four-wheeled trailer 90 mm long. It consists of a long, thin chassis carrying the two axles and one of two detachable separate pieces: a road scraper/snowplow blade and a hayrake. The main casting also includes a driver and steering wheel. It runs on four of the smaller six-spoked wheels (as on the front of the tractor), and its colors match those of the tractor in the set. Since the two trailers were issued only in these sets, and in one later one, they were never given numbers of their own.

Finally, 1928 brought the most modern aircraft model the firm had produced until then: the no. 4660 Aero-Dawn Monoplane. The name was meant to suggest that mankind was then at the very dawn of air travel, and was chosen after the firm learned that it could not legally use the name or even the registration number, NX 211, of Charles Lindbergh's *Spirit of St. Louis*, after which the Aero-Dawn had been patterned. So the 100 mm fuselage bore number UX 214 instead, and included a detailed nine-cylinder radial engine with a cast propeller. The 96 mm wings are a single tinplate piece with tabs that fit into slots in the fuselage. Two pairs of struts integral with the fuselage hold the axle with its two small metal wheels.

Despite the financial chaos of 1929, the year was one of progress for the Dowst firm. The Aero-Dawn's popularity inspired the production of a very similar biplane, no. 4675, named Wings after a popular motion picture of the time. Trouble came not from Hollywood, but from Parker Brothers, who produced a game with the same name, but the dispute was resolved and Dowst continued to supply Parker with diecast playing pieces for their games.

The fuselage of Wings is, at 96 mm, slightly shorter than that of the Aero-Dawn, but the wingspan, also 96 mm, is exactly the same. The wings differ though, in being two pieces, each with the upper and lower wing halves for one side of the plane, with a vertical panel connecting them and providing tabs to attach the wing pieces to the fuselage. Both planes remained in production until World War II and were used in numerous boxed sets, sometimes with tinplate pontoons in place of their wheels which, toward the end, were metal hubs with rubber tires. No separate numbers are known for the seaplanes, as they were probably not issued except in sets.

Inevitably, 1929 brought a Model A Ford Sedan, no. 6665. It consists of a 68 mm body casting, separate radiator/headlights casting identical to that of the Coupe, and the same four metal wheels with raised spokes. Unlike the Coupe, it has a rear spare wheel cover with the Ford name cast on it. Both Coupe and Sedan appeared in red, green and blue; the Sedan was also painted yellow and the Coupe tan, the latter used as a staff car in military sets. Both Fords were withdrawn at the end of 1933.

NO. 6201 CHEVROLET ROADSTER REPRESENTS A 1926 CHEVROLET. IT WAS ISSUED IN 1927 AND IS 1/43 SCALE.

NO. 6306 OLDSMOBILE DELIVERY TRUCK, REPRESENTS A 1926 OLDSMOBILE, ISSUED IN 1927. 1/43 SCALE.

NO. 4655 MODEL A FORD COUPE, ISSUED IN 1928. THIS THREE-WINDOW COUPE IS 65 MM, 1/48 SCALE.

HUBER FARM TRAILER FROM THE NO. 5010 FARM SET THAT WAS ISSUED IN 1928.

HUBER STAR ROAD SCRAPER, FROM THE NO. 7003 FARM SET ISSUED IN 1928.

The Safety Coach also gained a companion in 1929, the no. 4680 Overland Bus. The name does not denote the products of the Willys-Overland firm, which last used that name in 1926, but rather the OVERLAND BUS LINE lettering on the model. Unlike the Safety Coach, this model is not a single casting, but has a separate radiator/headlights casting. It differs in the rear, too, having an open observation platform, and its roof has three square raised panels. Like the Safety Coach, it ran on Disteel wheels and was made through 1933.

The Mack Truck series, which had been updated in 1928, was expanded in 1929 with the production of two semi-trailer vans, each consisting of the chassis/cab casting of the earlier trucks plus a two-wheeled semi-trailer unit. The latter is a closed box with a triangular front tab ending in a peg that fits into one of the holes in the cab's rear chassis. Two types were made, apparently both numbered 4670: a red A & P and a green Railway Express trailer. They were produced through 1932, and around 1931 a boxed set appeared with both trailers but only one cab.

Finally, several Playtime Sets were made around 1929. The lowest-priced type sold for $1.00 and held eleven models, including the Aero-Dawn, the Farm Tractor, a bus, five assorted cars and one other piece which may have been a fire truck. The $1.50 set included sixteen pieces, among them two planes and two fire trucks; the $2.00 set had twenty-one pieces and the $3.50 set had twenty-eight.

Only one new Tootsietoy appeared in 1930: the Ford Trimotor plane, issued first in a set and designated no. 4649 only in 1932 when it was sold individually. Bigger than the earlier aircraft (97 mm long, 132 mm wingspan), it is also more complex. Its main casting includes the fuselage, tail and central engine, while a second casting provides the other two engines, the landing gear, and various struts to connect them and fit around the fuselage. The wings are a single tinplate piece, with tabs that hold the plane together, while the three propellers and two wheels are of cast metal. The Trimotor was in production until the late thirties and was used in several sets, including the no. 5100 Airport Set which introduced it. This set contained two Trimotors and a tinplate hangar.

Aircraft suggested air mail, and in 1931 two mail trucks were issued, intended primarily for use with the planes in sets. One was a Mack Bulldog chassis/cab with a boxy rear body including screen side panels and U.S. MAIL/Air Mail Service lettering. The 76 mm model was usually if not always painted red (chassis) and tan (box), held together by the usual two rivets, and equipped with Disteel wheels. Numbered 4645, it was produced through 1933.

The other mail truck was a Model A Ford, 66 mm long, that had no number because it was available only in a boxed set. Its construction is much like that of the Coupe and Sedan, with a separate unpainted grille casting and spoked metal wheels; its rear body is that of a panel van with black U.S. MAIL lettering on the sides and two doors with screened windows at the rear. Apart from its grille and lettering it was painted a medium green, lighter than the Coupe and Sedan. It was used only in the no. 5041 Air Mail Set, which included two Ford and two Mack mail trucks, two Aero-Dawns, a Ford Trimotor, an airport pylon and six men. The set was withdrawn at the end of 1933, and the mail vans went with it.

The effect of the Great Depression was seen in 1931 in the form of small-scale models made to sell for five cents instead of the usual ten. Three models in a series of what later became ten were issued in 1931, each in a tinplate garage at first. The no. 4656 Coupe and 4657 Sedan represent Buick-built Marquettes of 1930; each is a single casting, 58 mm long, with four cast-metal wheels similar to the Model A Ford type but smaller. The bodies lack such details as headlights which would have made casting more complicated and expensive. The Buicks' only companion at first was a small open Mack fire truck or, officially, Insurance Patrol, no. 4658, likewise a single casting, almost the same size (59 mm), with the same wheels. The hood bears no monogram but is obviously a Mack; the rear body includes pieces of firefighting equipment. The series was expanded two years later.

Depression or not, the production of larger models continued, including a truck far

NO. 4660 AERO-DAWN
MONOPLANE, ISSUED IN
1928. FUSELAGE IS 100 MM
LONG AND WINGS ARE 96
MM ACROSS.

NO. 6665 MODEL A FORD SE-
DAN, ISSUED IN 1929.
REPRESENTS THE 1928
MODEL A, 1/48 SCALE AND
68 MM.

NO. 4680 OVERLAND BUS, IS-
SUED IN 1929. REPRESENTS
A 1926 OVERLAND. 1/72
SCALE.

NO. 4670 MACK TRAILER
TRUCK: A & P. ISSUED IN
1929, CAB IS A 1921 MACK
AC. 1/72 SCALE.

NO. 4670 MACK TRAILER
TRUCK: AMERICAN RAILWAY
EXPRESS.

longer than any previous Tootsietoy: the no. 190 Mack Auto Transport. The Bulldog chassis was modified to include a peg rising from a lowered rear surface; the peg fit through a hole in the front of a tinplate semi-trailer made to carry three small Buicks. Low side channels hold the cars' wheels, and a tab at each end keeps them aboard. The 215 mm truck was issued first with Disteel wheels, which were changed in 1933, shortly before its withdrawal, to rubber-tired metal hubs. It was sold with two Buick Sedans and one Coupe, though one often sees pictures of the truck with the Buick Roadster of 1933 in place of one of the Sedans.

Two military Macks, the first army models made by the firm, also appeared in 1931. Like the Auto Transport, they used a second-type Mack chassis/cab unit, but this particular casting, while including the Mack monogram and drive chains, had no door handles or hinges. The no. 4643 truck carries a two-piece anti-aircraft gun, its base attached to the chassis by a rivet that allows it to swivel, while the gun casting pivots vertically on two pins that attach it to the arms of the base. A similar system is used on the no. 4644 Searchlight Truck, where the light pivots vertically and the base swivels horizontally. These two trucks remained in production until the war. They were at first painted khaki and ran on Disteel wheels; later they were given metal hubs, rubber tires and a green and tan camouflage pattern. Just before the war, solid rubber wheels were used. The anti-aircraft gun was usually silver, the searchlight red or green; both bases were painted black. Each model is 70 mm long.

The no. 4647 Army Tank joined the Macks in the same year. Described as a "reproduction in miniature of the latest type Caterpillar Tank from specifications furnished by the U.S. Govt. War Dept.," it is actually a World War I Renault FT-17 tank. Its camouflage paint was originally red and black, later tan and green. A 79 mm single casting, it was fitted with four cast-metal hubs including ridges that fit into grooves on the insides of its rubber treads. It was still in production when the war brought toymaking to a halt.

A Long Range Cannon, no. 4642, lasted even longer, as it was reissued after the war. This 95 mm model consists of two castings: the chassis, which includes a towing hook, axle holes, holes for the cannon's pivoting pegs, and a large shield with a hole for the cannon's barrel; and the cannon itself, which has a hollow barrel with spring and lever that let it fire small projectiles. At first the gun was painted silver and the chassis red, and it ran on large eight-spoked metal wheels. Later the colors were changed to olive and khaki and the wheels to large black rubber ones with eight raised spokes. The Cannon was used in numerous sets, usually with an adapted Farm Tractor or another 1931 issue, the Caterpillar Tractor, to pull it. Some sets included a Mortar, offered separately in 1933 as no. 4662, with a shorter, thicker barrel and without the Cannon's shield. It first appeared in the no. 5071 Field Battery Set issued in 1931.

The no. 4646 Caterpillar Tractor, though used in some military sets, was basically a civilian vehicle. It shared with the Army Tank the ridged metal hubs and grooved rubber treads, and the distinction of being the first Tootsietoys equipped with them. The 77 mm single casting includes driver and hitching loop as well as the usual body details, and bears a diamond-shaped emblem enclosing a capital T—not, as has been theorized, for Diamond T, as that truck manufacturer did not produce heavy equipment, but for Tootsietoys. The model was painted red for civilian use, khaki or olive when used in military sets, and was produced until the war.

A short-lived model despite having more personality than the Caterpillar was the no. 4648 Steam Roller, which lasted only through 1934. It is actually a model of an early diesel-powered roller. Its main casting includes a four-pillared roof over the driver's seat, but no driver. A second casting, attached at the front and pivoting on its rivet, consists of two arms that hold the wooden roller. Two eight-spoked metal wheels complete the 73 mm model, which was painted a light red with silver or black wheels and roller.

NO. 4649 FORD TRIMOTOR, ISSUED IN 1930 IN A SET. NUMBER WAS DESIGNATED IN 1932 WHEN IT WAS SOLD INDIVIDUALLY. 97 MM LONG, 132 MM WINGSPAN.

NO. 4645 MACK MAIL TRUCK, ISSUED IN 1931, WAS A MODEL OF A 1921 MACK AC BULLDOG. 1/72 SCALE, 76 MM.

MODEL A FORD MAIL TRUCK (UNNUMBERED) REP-RESENTS A 1928 FORD MODEL A SEDAN DELIVERY, ISSUED IN 1931. 1/48 SCALE, 66 MM. AVAILABLE ONLY IN BOXED SET.

NO. 190 AUTO TRANSPORT HAULING: NO. 102 BUICK ROADSTER, NO. 101 BUICK COUPE AND NO. 103 BUICK SEDAN. THE 58 MM (1/72 SCALE) BUICKS WERE MODELED AFTER 1930 MAR-QUETTES AND WERE ISSUED IN 1932. THE TRANSPORT, A 1921 MACK AC, WAS FIRST ISSUED IN 1931 AND IS 215 MM, 1/43 SCALE.

NO. 4643 MACK ANTI-AIR-CRAFT GUN TRUCK. THE MACK IS A 1921 AC. ISSUED IN 1931, THE MODEL IS 1/72 SCALE, 70 MM.

The new models of 1931 found their way into numerous sets. The no. 5071 Field Battery Set, with three Cannons, three Mortars and two modified Farm Tractors, was one of three military sets issued then. The changes to the tractor casting include not only the towing loop but also a rear-mounted ammunition box with U.S. ARMY lettering. It was painted khaki, used only in this set, and withdrawn along with the conventional Tractor at the end of 1932. The Field Battery Set also included six soldiers.

The Aerial Offense and Aerial Defense Sets appeared at the same time. The former contained three Ford Trimotors, four other planes which may be Aero-Dawns, and six men; the latter held three planes (apparently Aero-Dawns again), two Searchlight and two Anti-Aircraft Gun Trucks, a scout car (a G.M. coupe, probably the Buick, painted a solid tan), and the same six men. Both sets were produced through 1933.

The two older farm sets were blended into a single one composed of the Tractor, box trailer, road scraper, hayrake and Model T Truck. It was withdrawn at the end of 1932, along with all its components. A Motor Set—with various cars, a G.M. Delivery Truck and a plane—and a Playtime Toys Set of nine assorted vehicles were also offered in 1931; both were continued the next year with changes in their contents. Finally, two railroad sets blended existing pieces and new issues. The Midnight Flyer Set offered the usual Locomotive, Tender and Pullman Coach, plus a new Baggage Car and Observation Car much resembling the Pullman. The Fast Freight Set used the Locomotive, Tender and Gondola along with two new freight cars: a Boxcar lettered TOOTSIETOY R R 004695 and a Caboose with the same name and number 4697. If these cars were issued individually, 4695 and 4697 were probably their numbers.

The following year, 1932, brought the immortal Funnies Set, no. 5091. Its six pieces were issued individually in comparatively simple form as well as in the set, where they had more elaborate color schemes and also eccentric cams on their axles to make the comic-strip figures in them bob up and down as the models rolled. A look at the paint and the axles, then, will suffice to tell the two types apart: if the entire figure casting is one color and there is no cam on the axle, the model was issued individually.

The first of the six, no. 5101, is Andy Gump's Car. The stubby open roadster is 70 mm long, has number 348 license plates on its grille and tail, and runs on large cast-metal wheels. The car was painted red, the wheels green and black. The figure casting, painted orange in the simpler version, includes chinless Andy, a blob of a steering wheel, and either two axle holes or, in the boxed-set version, one hole and a bar that rides on the other axle's cam to make Andy bob up and down.

Uncle Walt's Car, no. 5102, is a longer, slimmer roadster, 82 mm long, with license number 354. The green car runs on red and black disc wheels like those used on the 23 Racer and the fire trucks. It is a more realistic car than Andy's, and the same applies to its driver. Uncle Walt's casting, painted orange in the simpler version, hooks over the dashboard and either has a hole for the rear axle or is mounted on a pin and activated by the rear axle's cam.

Smitty's Motorcycle, no. 5103, includes not only Smitty cast integrally with the 78 mm cycle, but also Herbie in the sidecar. The cycle is realistic, with a well-detailed four-cylinder engine; its driver is attired in cap and leathers. The sleek sidecar is a separate casting, and so is Herbie, who is held in a rectangular aperture by a pin uniting the front of the sidecar and the cycle and by the rear axle which holds the cycle's rear wheel and the single wheel of the sidecar. The three wheels are a large, spoked metal-type used nowhere else; they are painted silver, the cycle and sidecar are yellow, and Herbie seems to have been unpainted. This is the most complex model in the series, and the only one that was put to another use after the Funnies Set was withdrawn.

Next comes the no. 5104 Police Wagon, 73 mm long, driven by a helmeted officer and carrying a standing figure of Moon Mullins. The driver's seat and the rear floor are cut away

NO. 4644 MACK SEARCH-
LIGHT TRUCK, ISSUED IN
1931. 1/72 SCALE, 70 MM.

NO. 4647 ARMY TANK. DE-
SCRIBED IN BROCHURES AS
A CATERPILLAR TANK, IT IS
ACTUALLY A RENAULT. IS-
SUED IN 1931. 1/48 SCALE, 79
MM.

NO. 4642 LONG RANGE CAN-
NON, ISSUED IN 1931. WAS
USED IN NUMEROUS SETS.
95 MM.

NO. 4646 CATERPILLAR
TRACTOR, ISSUED IN 1931.
1/48 SCALE, 77 MM.

to make room for the figure casting, which includes both men, a bar to connect them, and another to the rear axle or cam. The silver wheels are like those on Andy Gump's Car, the body of the vehicle is blue, and the figure casting is brown; but despite the somber hues, the insouciant figure of Moon standing precariously in the back gives the model a vivid personality.

The no. 5105 Ice Wagon inevitably carries Kayo. The 74 mm truck is brown and unspectacular, with a closed cab, a load of ice blocks, and space on its tailboard for a sitting figure of Kayo, scarcely noticeable under his derby hat. Mounted on a pin behind the rear axle, he is unable to do much bobbing on the action version. Kayo is painted red, and the wheels, similar to those of the Police Wagon but smaller, are orange, probably with black treads. The insignificance of Kayo's small seated figure makes this the dullest of the six models.

Last but certainly not least is the no. 5106 rowboat issued under the name of Uncle Willie but bearing on its bow the name of its other passenger, Mamie. The boat's deck consists of bow and stern sections with the wheels underneath, plus a small section between the two figures, who are linked by a bar under it. Uncle Willie sits forward, with a pin holding his end of the figure casting in place. Mamie is behind him, and the figure casting extends to the rear axle or cam, which means that in the action version Mamie does much more bobbing than Willie. The boat is a light cream color; the figure casting is orange. The wheels, or rollers as they might be called, are unpainted and out of sight.

The Funnies models were not a commercial success and were withdrawn at the end of 1933, which accounts for their rarity today. It is ironic that these six models, so prized and valuable today, were a failure in their own time, and that their failure along with that of the Buck Rogers Rocket Ships several years later discouraged the firm from making any similar models.

Another 1932 issue was the no. 4666 Racer that is actually quite a good model of Malcolm Campbell's Bluebird I, which held the world's land speed record for a time in 1928. Though it was described as "the world's fastest racer, " it was never identified as the Bluebird or painted blue, for other firms had been authorized to make models of the Bluebird. A single casting 95 mm long, it includes considerable body detail, exhaust pipes, side-mounted radiators, a diamond-shaped TT emblem, and a cockpit with a featureless driver's head. The model was usually painted red when sold separately; it ran at first on the plain disc wheels used on the 23 Racer, and later on rubber tires on metal hubs. It remained in production until 1941 and was used in a truly remarkable set.

This was the no. 5081 Speedway Set, actually a game consisting of a rolled paper sheet with an oval race track printed on it, a spinner to determine the movement of the cars, and eight racers, each painted a different color and bearing a different number on its tailfin. Using the speed record car in a track race is unthinkable enough—to toy manufacturers any car that goes fast, or looks as if it does, is a racer—but to make things worse, each car was given the name of a different make of racing or sports car and a different old-time driver:

1. Stutz Bearcat, Cooper, cream.
2. Duesenberg Spl., DePaolo, red.
3. Marmon Spl., Harroun, yellow.
4. Packard Spl., DePalma, gold.
5. Blitzen Benz, Oldfield, lilac.
6. Studebaker Champion, Milton, silver.
7. Peugot [sic] Spl., Goux, green.
8. National, Wilcox, orange.

While the car names are for the most part those of track racing cars (the Stutz Bearcat was a sports roadster, though Stutz did build some very successful racing cars, and the Studebaker racing cars of the twenties were actually Millers), they do not always match with the drivers'

NO. 4648 STEAM ROLLER, IS-
SUED IN 1931. 73 MM.

NO. 5101 ANDY GUMP CAR,
ISSUED 1932. 70 MM.

NO. 5102 UNCLE WALT CAR,
ISSUED 1932. 82 MM.

NO. 5103 SMITTY MOTOR-
CYCLE AND SIDECAR, IS-
SUED 1932. 78 MM.

NO. 5104 MOON MULLINS
POLICE WAGON, ISSUED
1932. 73 MM.

names (Milton and the Studebaker, and Wilcox and the National, seem to be marriages of convenience), and neither all the cars nor all the drivers would be found on a track at the same time (Ray Harroun retired a good ten years before Peter DePaolo began to race). Some of the colors are ghastly (would even Barney Oldfield have driven a purple Blitzen Benz?), and the effect of it all is enough to convulse anyone who knows old-time auto racing—not that the game was made with such people in mind!

In 1932 the series of small-scale, low-cost models begun two years before was expanded to its full extent of ten pieces. The three existing vehicles were given new numbers: the Buick Marquette Coupe and Sedan became 101 and 103, and the Insurance Patrol 104; and the tinplate garages were dropped. The first new member of the series was the no. 102 Buick Roadster, similar in its basic details to the Coupe and Sedan, with tombstone grille and rear spare, plus a detailed open cab with a folded top behind it. Like the other Buicks, it is 58 mm long and painted a solid red, yellow, green or blue.

A second Mack truck appeared, but, unlike the fire truck, the no. 105 Tank Truck was a closed Mack. It is 59 mm long, apparently always painted green, and its tank is divided into three sections, each with a filler cap. The cab, unlike the roofed but open Bulldog cab, was completely enclosed.

Two small monoplanes were included in the series, each with a single fuselage casting, a metal propeller, small metal wheels and a single tinplate piece to provide the wings. No. 106 has its wings below the fuselage; those of no. 107 are mounted above. Neither is anywhere near as interesting as the Aero-Dawn or the Ford Trimotor.

The no. 108 Caterpillar Tractor, 52 mm long, is by no means identical to its big brother. It is a smaller, narrower vehicle, and though it has a seat and a steering wheel, it lacks a driver. It has a towing loop, but there was nothing in the Tootsietoy line at that time that it could have towed. Its treads and hubs are quite unlike those of the big Caterpillar, for the hubs are concave and the treads ride in their hollows much like rubber tires. The tractor was painted red or orange, with black hubs.

The no. 109 Stake Truck's radiator identifies it as a Ford. Its cab is enclosed; behind it is a solid panel on each side bearing a diamond-shaped TT emblem like that on the Bluebird. The stake sides begin aft of these panels, and a low tailboard forms the rear of the truck. The length is 57 mm, the color is usually yellow or red.

The series ends with no. 110, a small (68 mm) version of the Bluebird—or, formally, Racer. Its details are roughly like its big sister, but simpler, and it is noticeably shorter and stubbier. It lacks exhaust pipes, and its cockpit is open and empty. It was painted white or cream, and used the same small spoked wheels as the rest of the series. These ten models were produced through 1934, then replaced by a new series of small cars.

A Miniatures Set of ten pieces, including two planes, the large Racer, the large Caterpillar, and assorted cars and trucks, was available in 1932, and the Motor Set and Playtime Toys Set of the previous year were revised. The Funnies and the small series had made 1932 memorable, but 1933 would be even more so.

That remarkable year brought not only Zamak, rubber tires and the deletion of most of the older Tootsietoy models, but also two superb series subsidized by manufacturers of the vehicles they represented. Along with this, Ted Dowst and his crew did a good job of designing and producing the models that influenced the toy business around the world.

The makers of Mack trucks, noting the popularity of the earlier Mack models, supported the preparation of a new series of trucks composed for the most part of three castings: the truck cab, with monogrammed hood and radiator (between hood and cab); the chassis and front fenders; and the rear body or semi-trailer unit. The cab is fully enclosed, with door windows of a curious shape, nearly circular but with a straight diagonal line at the front. A tab at the rear of the cab hooks into a slot in the chassis, while front axle tabs project through two other slots, so that the front axle and rear tab hold the two pieces together. Axle holes in the

NO. 5105 KAYO ICE WAGON, MARKED KO ON THE CASTING, ISSUED IN 1932. 74 MM.

NO. 5106 UNCLE WILLIE BOAT, ISSUED 1932.

NO. 4666 RACER. KNOWN AS THE LARGER OF TWO BLUE-BIRD MODELS, IT WAS NEVER IDENTIFIED AS SUCH IN LITERATURE. ISSUED IN 1932, 95 MM LONG.

NO. 105 MACK TANK TRUCK AND NO. 4658 MACK INSURANCE PATROL. THE FORMER WAS ISSUED IN 1932; THE LATTER IN 1931. BOTH ARE 59 MM AND REPRESENT 1930 MACK AC BULLDOGS.

NO. 106 LOW WING MONOPLANE, ISSUED IN 1932.

chassis carry the rear axle, and the chassis also includes a hitching pin for a semi-trailer or rivets for a rear body.

The first of the new Macks, no. 801, is a Stake Trailer Truck. Its trailer is a single casting with flat bed, semicircular front wall, and sides and back of bars and stakes, except for a panel on each side with the word EXPRESS. Two axle tabs descend at the rear, and the single axle, like the rear axle of the cab, carries dual wheels, giving the model a total of ten rubber-tired metal hubs. The truck was painted a solid red or green except for the black chassis, and measured 137 mm. Along with almost all the other Macks, it was revised in 1936 to have a single-casting cab unit and single wheels all around, eliminating the dual wheels and the black chassis. In this form it lasted through 1941.

The no. 802 Oil Trailer Truck is a semi-trailer rig 138 mm long. A tinplate tank is attached to its diecast trailer chassis by tabs through chassis slots. The logo bears the name DOMACO (obviously coined from *DO*wst *MA*nufacturing *CO*mpany), with GASOLINE AND OILS beneath it in smaller letters. Two color schemes were used: green cab and trailer with red tank, or orange cab and trailer with red tank. The lettering is black, as is the first-type chassis. Wheels are as on the Stake Truck. The revised model was produced through 1941.

Number 803 is a Van Trailer Truck, 139 mm long, often named by collectors for its LONG DISTANCE HAULING logo. The trailer casting is a large box with no top and a low tailgate. A tinplate top slides over ridges along the top of the box, and a small casting is attached under the trailer to hold two small metal wheels on which the trailer rests when uncoupled from the cab. Unlike the other semi-trailers, it is not rounded but square in front. The truck as a whole is heavy and bulky, and its complexity must have made it expensive to produce. Not surprisingly, it was dropped at the end of 1936, so that its second version, with one-piece cab and single wheels all around, is quite rare. The truck was painted green, with a red or unpainted tinplate trailer roof, and the first version had the usual black chassis.

The first non-articulated truck in the series is no. 804, a heavy Coal Truck 100 mm long, with yellow cab, black first-type chassis and green rear body. The latter is a sturdy open box, riveted to the chassis, with CITY FUEL COMPANY lettering in two lines on each side, and with a pair of axle tabs on the bottom, beyond the end of the chassis, to carry the second of the truck's two rear axles. The first type has dual wheels on both axles for a total of ten. The rare second version, made from 1936 through 1938, has only one rear axle, the rearmost one, with single wheels. This heavy truck looks not only unreal but truly pathetic with four wheels and empty axle holes, its strength and dignity all but lost.

The no. 805 Milk Trailer Truck brings us back to semi-trailers and measures 145 mm. Unlike the massive Domaco tanker, it has a light trailer chassis, little more than a horizontal ledge with a fragile stake rail all around and slots for the tabs of the tinplate tank. A towing loop at the back enables it to pull a full trailer, which it did in a subsequent set, and two tabs carry the single axle with, in the first version, dual wheels. The tin tank, identical to that of the Domaco truck, is painted white with black TOOTSIE TOY DAIRY lettering. The rest of the truck, except for the black first-type chassis, is yellow. The truck remained in production as no. 805 through 1939, but was used in the no. 192 Milk Trailers Set until 1941.

The next Mack, numbered 190X to distinguish it from the earlier three-car carrier, is a longer Auto Transport with a tinplate semi-trailer made to carry four small Buicks. The whole model is 272 mm long and was sold with a load of two Buick Sedans and two Coupes. Painted red save for the black first-type chassis, it was withdrawn at the end of 1936, making its second version quite rare.

An anomaly of sorts is the no. 191 Contractor Set. Its cab body is a different casting from the others: it extends in a low box to the back of the chassis, with its rear panel cut away to give access to a towing loop on the chassis. Four axle tabs pass through slots in the chassis, and the axles unite the two castings. Thus both pieces were made for this model alone, and a second type was never made, but neither was it ever issued with dual wheels. The four

NO. 110 SMALL RACER, IS-
SUED IN 1932; IS 68 MM
LONG. NO. 108 CATERPILLAR
TRACTOR, ISSUED IN 1932;
1/87 SCALE, 52 MM.

NO. 801 MACK STAKE TRAIL-
ER TRUCK, 1/43 SCALE, 137
MM. FIRST IN THE SERIES OF
MACK TRUCKS THAT WERE
ISSUED IN 1933, ALL OF
WHICH REPRESENTED 1932
AC BULLDOGS.

NO. 802 MACK OIL TRAILER
TRUCK, ISSUED 1933. 1/43
SCALE, 138 MM.

NO. 803 MACK VAN TRAILER
TRUCK, ISSUED 1933. 1/43
SCALE, 139 MM.

NO. 804 MACK COAL TRUCK,
ISSUED 1933. 1/43 SCALE,
100 MM.

rubber tires on the cab are, in fact, the only ones on the model, for the cab pulls three side-tipping trailers consisting of diecast tippers, sheet-metal chassis and spoked metal wheels. The cab unit and trailer chassis and wheels are black; the tippers are usually three different bright colors such as red, orange and pale green. They may not look real, but they do brighten up the model. The total length is 311 mm. The model was produced through 1941.

The Tootsietoy Dairy Tanker reappeared in the no. 192 set, which consisted of the no. 805 Milk Trailer Truck plus two full trailers similar in construction to the semi-trailer. The trailers have front hooks and rear towing loops, two pairs of axle tabs, and the first-version trailers had dual wheels front and back, giving the model a total of twenty-six wheels, while the second type had fourteen. Construction and color details are like those of no. 805, and the entire set, which was produced through 1941, measures 337 mm.

No other Macks were issued in 1933, though the series was expanded later. One other commercial vehicle did appear that year: the no. 807 Delivery Cycle, a modified form of Smitty's Motorcycle from the Funnies Set. Smitty and his cycle were unchanged, but Herbie and his sidecar were replaced by a diecast box with a raising lid, attached to the cycle as before by a pin at the front of the box and by the rear axle. The same big, spoked wheels were used, and the model, still 76 mm long, was painted red with the driver's clothing (except for his red cap) black and his face flesh-colored. The model was produced only in 1933.

The makers of Mack trucks were not alone in subsidizing new Tootsietoys in 1933. They were joined by the manufacturers of Graham automobiles, and the models of 1932-33 Graham Blue Streak cars became classics of their kind. These models introduced the three-part construction that was copied by numerous other makers of miniature cars. The smallest of the three pieces is the radiator, which also includes the headlights and front bumper. It attaches to the body, as usual, by a rivet on its back. The bodies, which we shall discuss individually, have four axle tabs that pass through slots in the chassis, and the two axles hold the model together. The chassis includes the fenders, running boards, taillights and rear bumper. Two basic types were made, one with and the other without spare wheel wells in the front fenders. Another type of chassis, made for use in the Bild-a-Car Set, has widened axle channels to hold a central sleeve that connects two half-axles but allows them to be removed so bodies and chassis can be switched. The Grahams were issued with rubber tires on metal hubs until 1941, when the last of the models appeared with solid rubber wheels.

The Graham body types issued in 1933 include a roadster, coupe, sedan, town car, wrecker and dairy van. Later a tire van and an ambulance were added. The roadster, coupe, sedan and town car bodies were made with either an attachment place for a single spare wheel at the rear or pinholes for twin side-mounted spares; all but the town car were also made with no spare. The four-wheel (i.e., no spare wheel) roadster, sedan and coupe were used only in sets, while the five-wheel and six-wheel types were sold individually. The chassis with wheel wells was used for the six-wheel types; the rear spare of the five-wheel versions required no chassis modification.

Numerically the Graham Roadster comes first; it is no. 511 in five-wheel and 611 in six-wheel form, both versions being in production through 1935, while the unnumbered four-wheel type was used in sets through 1937. The two-door body includes a detailed interior and open rumble seat. The body casting also has two slots into which a separate windshield/dashboard/steering-wheel casting fits.

The Coupe exists in five versions: no. 512 in five-wheel and 612 in six-wheel form (1933-35), the unnumbered four-wheel type used in sets through 1939, and the 514 five-wheel and 614 six-wheel Convertible Coupe versions, in which the top and back of the roof are painted tan to simulate canvas. Like their conventional counterparts, the Convertibles were available individually through 1935. Since the Grahams were usually painted in contrasting chassis and body colors, the tan convertible top gives these models a three-color finish.

NO. 190X AUTO TRANSPORT, CARRIED FOUR CARS COMPARED TO THE THREE-CAR CAPACITY OF THE EARLIER MACK AC TRANSPORT (NO. 190). ISSUED IN 1933, THIS ONE IS 272 MM LONG. IN BACK ARE THE NO. 109 FORD STAKE TRUCK, 57 MM; NO. 101 BUICK COUPE, 58 MM; NO. 102 BUICK ROADSTER, 58 MM; AND NO. 103 BUICK SEDAN, 58 MM.

NO. 191 CONTRACTOR SET, ISSUED IN 1933. CONSISTED OF A 1932 MACK AC HAULING THREE SIDE-TIPPERS. TOTAL LENGTH IS 311 MM.

NO. 192 MILK TRAILERS SET CONSISTED OF NO. 805 MILK TRAILER TRUCK, 145 MM (A 1932 MACK AC), HERE SHOWN WITH THREE TRAILERS (THE ORIGINAL SET CONTAINED ONLY TWO). 1/43 SCALE.

NO. 807 DELIVERY CYCLE WAS ISSUED IN 1933. IT IS 76 MM LONG.

UNNUMBERED TOURING CAR RESEMBLES A 1926 OAKLAND; IT WAS ISSUED IN 1933. 1/43 SCALE.

The same five types of the Sedan exist: no. 513 five-wheel, no. 613 six-wheel, un-numbered four-wheel, no. 515 five-wheel Convertible and no. 615 six-wheel Convertible. All were produced through 1935, and the four-wheel type was used in sets through 1939. As on the Coupe, body detail lines extend over the doors and side windows and then sweep down under the rear window to define the area painted tan on the convertibles. The Sedan was also used in a taxicab set with its body and chassis painted the same color, either orange or yellow. Except for their use in this and the Bild-a-Car Set, the Sedans were painted in two or, for the convertibles, three colors.

The Town Car was produced in only two forms, no. 516 five-wheel and 616 six-wheel; it was never issued without a spare tire and was withdrawn completely at the end of 1935. The rear part of the car is enclosed, while the driver's seat is open, and a windshield casting identical to that of the Roadster is used. Because of its short life span and infrequent use in sets, the Town Car is among the rarer Grahams.

The Graham Wrecker appeared in only one form, no. 806, with no spare wheel. It was produced through 1939. The enclosed two-door cab drops off sharply to a rear deck from which the crane boom rises. At the end of the boom a wire towing-hook is fitted. The Wrecker usually, if not always, was made with a black chassis and red body.

The last Graham issued in 1933 was the no. 808 Dairy Van, made in four-wheel form through 1939. Its roof and sides run smoothly back to form ninety-degree angles with each other and with the vertical rear panel which includes two doors with round windows. The logo takes the form of block capitals, with TOOTSIETOY above and DAIRY centered below it. The body was painted white or cream, the chassis black.

The other two Grahams, the Ambulance and Commercial Tire Van, were not issued until 1935. In 1933, though, several sets were offered that consist solely or partly of Grahams. The no. 5360 Bild-a-Car Set includes five Graham chassis with wide axle channels, five bodies, and enough wheels, half-axles and sleeves to equip five cars. Five different colors were used, with one body and one chassis painted each color, so that one could make up either solid-color or two-tone cars. Two Sedan and two Coupe bodies were used; the fifth body was at first (1933-37) that of a Roadster, but in 1938, the last year this set was sold, the Commercial Tire Van body was substituted. It is possible, then, for single-color Sedans, Coupes, Roadsters and Tire Vans to exist as four-wheel types with half-axles—possible but not very probable, as one seldom hears of any except an occasional Sedan or Coupe and, very rarely, an all-orange Tire Van.

The no. 5350 Taxicab Set also appeared in 1933; it was composed of four Sedans in four-wheel form, two painted yellow, the other two orange, and one Wrecker, presumably in its usual red and black. Since these single-color Sedans were issued complete, they can be told from the Bild-a-Car Sedans by their full axles. Though they were meant to represent taxis, they were never lettered or otherwise marked as such.

The no. 5300 Tootsietoy Motors Set included ten Grahams: a six-wheel and two five-wheel Coupes, the same assortment of Sedans, a five-wheel and a six-wheel Roadster, a six-wheel Town Car and a Wrecker. In 1935, the last year of this set's life, one of the ten (perhaps a Roadster or the Town Car?) was replaced by the new Commercial Tire Van, always with an orange body and brown chassis. Its body was like that of the Dairy Van, but the Commercial Tire Co. logo was much more ornate. When this set was discontinued, the Tire Van went into limbo until it was resurrected in 1938 for the Bild-a-Car Set, where it appeared with the usual orange body and a choice of five chassis, one also painted orange, another brown. The Tire Van never appeared outside of these two sets. Its origin can be told by its axle type, as those from the Motors Set had full axles.

The Dairy Van and Wrecker were used in the no. 5310 Truck Set available from 1933 through 1935, along with five different Mack trucks and the Delivery Cycle at first. In 1934 the Dairy Van and Delivery Cycle were replaced by the Ford Trimotor—a strange thing to

NO. 516 GRAHAM FIVE-WHEEL TOWN CAR AND NO. 611 GRAHAM SIX-WHEEL ROADSTER. ALL GRAHAM MODELS REPRESENT 1932 GRAHAM BLUE STREAKS. 1/43 SCALE, WERE ISSUED IN 1933.

NO. 512 GRAHAM FIVE-WHEEL COUPE, AND GRAHAM FOUR-WHEEL COUPE (NO NUMBER—FOUR-WHEEL-TYPE CARS WERE SOLD ONLY IN SETS).

GRAHAM FOUR-WHEEL SEDAN AND NO. 613 GRAHAM SIX-WHEEL SEDAN.

NO. 806 GRAHAM WRECKER.

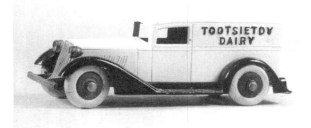

NO. 808 GRAHAM DAIRY VAN.

find in a Truck Set! Other changes were made in 1935, with the new Railway Express Van replacing an earlier Mack and the equally new Douglas DC-2 taking the Trimotor's place.

A new Battery Set, no. 197, was also made in 1933. Here the large Caterpillar took the place of the defunct army version of the Farm Tractor; it pulled a single Long Range Cannon manned by six soldiers. The set remained in production until the war, with the Cannon's wheels changing from spoked metal to solid black rubber along the way. Another set available in 1933 was called Aces of the Air and contained two Aero-Dawn and two Wings planes, one of each with pontoons instead of wheels.

Though some of the finest Tootsietoys of all time were still to come, there is no other year in Tootsietoy history that can equal 1933 in terms of quality and quantity of new issues. It was truly an incredible year. On the other hand, 1934 brought only one new model, though an unusual one: the no. 4659 Autogyro. (We assume that was its number; Mr. Lee lists it as 4650, but that was the Biplane's number, and as 4659 is otherwise unused, we believe the number given by Mr. Lee is a typographical error. The spelling of the name comes from Mr. Lee's article, too. The dictionary gives 'autogiro' as the first spelling, but this was used as a trade name; perhaps the firm used the second spelling to avoid difficulties.) The model's fuselage is a single casting, 99 mm long, with a five-cylinder radial engine in front, complete with cast-metal propeller, and the usual fin and stabilizers at the rear. Atop the fuselage is a tall, tapering tower to which the tinplate rotor blades are pinned; just behind this pillar is the cockpit, with the pilot's head cast in. The 108 mm wings are a single piece of tin, tilting up at each end. The wings slide onto the fuselage over the landing-gear struts, which include small tabs that can be crimped to hold the wings in place. At first the model was made with rubber tires on metal hubs; later solid rubber wheels were fitted. It was withdrawn from production late in the thirties.

The next year, 1935, brought another new Tootsietoy aircraft: the no. 717 Douglas DC-2 Airliner that remained in production until the war. Measuring 99 mm long with a wingspan of 135 mm, it is made of two castings joined internally. Each casting includes one side of the fuselage and one wing; the entire tail is part of the left-side casting. Each wing bears one engine nacelle, to which a three-bladed propeller is attached, and the plane's three small metal wheels are mounted below the nacelles and the tail. T W A is cast on the left wing, NC 101 Y on the right. The DC-2 and Autogyro were included in an Aeroplane Set that also contained a Ford Trimotor and the Wings and Aero-Dawn seaplanes.

In 1935 an interesting railroad vehicle was produced: the no. 117 Zephyr Railcar. It is a single casting, 97 mm long, with cast-in trucks at each end but only two actual solid rubber wheels on an axle mounted slightly forward of center, so that the car's rear rests on its cast-in trucks. The Zephyr name and the number 9900 are cast on each side of the car; other details include a large headlight, two small taillights, and a front section raised above the main roof level. The model was painted a single color; it was withdrawn after only two years.

The year of 1935 also brought several new Tootsietoy road vehicles, including the last two Grahams. The Commercial Tire Van, already discussed, was joined by the no. 809 Ambulance. The body of this model was much like those of the two vans; it features a raised red cross on each side. It was never issued with spare tires or half-axles, so its only variations are those of paint: its body was either white or cream, its chassis white or black. Later an army version appeared, either in solid khaki or green and tan camouflage. The Army Ambulance was used until the war, and at the end it appeared with solid rubber wheels in place of the usual rubber-tired metal hubs. Since it was used only in sets, it was not numbered.

The Grahams were outdone, both in elegant appearance and complex construction, by two other 1935 products, the rare and beautiful LaSalles. Larger than the Grahams, they are 108 mm long and consist of four pieces: body, chassis, a grille casting including headlights and front bumper, and a fourth piece forming the rear bumper. The grille is not riveted in place, but slides into slots in the body and is held there by the chassis. The rear bumper is

NO. 4659 AUTOGYRO. FUSE-
LAGE CASTING IS 99 MM. IS-
SUED IN 1934.

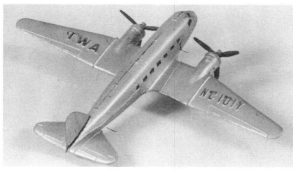

NO. 717 DOUGLAS DC-2
AIRLINER, ISSUED IN 1935.
LENGTH 99 MM, WINGSPAN
135 MM.

NO. 117 ZEPHYR RAILCAR,
ISSUED IN 1935. 97 MM.

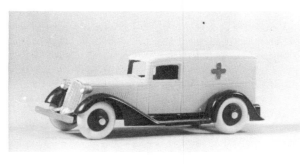

NO. 809 GRAHAM
AMBULANCE, ISSUED IN
1935. 1/43 SCALE.

NO. 809 GRAHAM ARMY
AMBULANCE, WITH 1941
SOLID RUBBER WHEELS.

held in place by two tabs that lock between the body and chassis, which in turn hook together at the rear and are united at the front by the axle running through tabs that pass through the chassis.

The LaSalle Coupe appeared in two forms, no. 712 with either solid-color or two-tone paint, and no. 714, the Convertible Coupe, with a tan roof panel. The Sedan took two forms as well, no. 713 in conventional and 715 in convertible paint. Body detail is excellent; a long, slim hood tapers to the narrow grille, while panels flare out on each side to fill the space between the hood and the fenders. No spare wheels are carried, but even so, the LaSalles combine regal stateliness and sleek, exciting beauty. Though the regular Coupe and Sedan were produced through 1939 and the convertibles through 1936, very few have survived, and now they bring three-figure prices when one can find them for sale at all. There are rarer Tootsietoys, but the LaSalles have made their name synonymous with rarity, desirability—and high price.

In 1935 the Tootsietoy firm sought to duplicate the success of its Model A Ford by preparing a model of a prototype made for Ford Motors by the Briggs Manufacturing Company. The project eventually gave birth to the Lincoln Zephyr, but only after the Ford-Briggs relationship had come to an abrupt end, leaving the firm with expensive dies for a model of a car that never existed. As Mr. Lee points out, the prototype had a single large door on the left and two doors on the right, while the model has two doors on each side, as the firm probably assumed the production car would have. Since the dies existed, they were put to use, but the model needed a name. It was then that Ted Dowst is said to have made his classic statement, "We make toys for doodling, not models for collecting." So the model was named Doodlebug, numbered 716, and produced through at least late 1936 and probably part of 1937.

The Doodlebug was made in a new type of three-part construction. Car styles were changing, and the Briggs prototype's fenders were faired into its body, so there was no need for a separate chassis casting. A single body unit, 102 mm long, includes skirted rear fenders with axle holes, and front axle pillars inboard of open fenders. The second casting includes a tall rectangular grille, headlights and a front bumper; the third provides the rear bumper plus two taillights that protrude through holes in the rear fenders. Both castings are attached to the body by rivets that pass through inner body tabs. The usual white rubber tires and metal hubs are used, and since the rear wheels are inside the fender skirts, the rear axle is crimped in two places to keep the wheels from sliding toward each other.

The styling of the Doodlebug, like that of many futuristic cars, was no rival for the lovely Grahams and LaSalles. The thoroughbreds' classic lines gave way to a fastback style that was sleek and smooth, yet at the same time dumpy and graceless. The model was not a good seller, and was later changed for cheaper production, better esthetics and greater fidelity to the car that finally grew out of the Briggs project.

The big, homely Doodlebug was joined in 1935 by a smaller and simpler but scarcely more handsome model, the no. 118 DeSoto Airflow. This model, which was to become part of a new series of low-priced models, is a single casting, 76 mm long, with small white rubber wheels. Like the Doodlebug, it has rear fender skirts with axle holes, open front fenders and pillars to hold the front axle. At first the car was painted in one basic color with silver trim; later the trim was eliminated, and at times the entire model was painted silver. It remained in production through 1939.

Joining the Airflow in what was to become a large series of small, low-cost models were three 1934 Fords—a sedan, coupe and wrecker—of two-piece construction. The no. 111 Sedan and no. 112 Coupe, each 76 mm long, portrayed the down-to-earth Ford V-8 cars of the day, and each was issued in convertible form with a tan roof, the Convertible Coupe being no. 114 and the Convertible Sedan no. 115. In the middle of the line was the no. 113 Ford Wrecker, its boom making it, at 81 mm, the longest of the Fords. Each model consists of

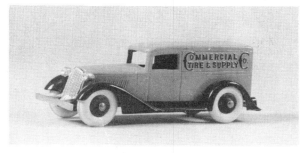

GRAHAM COMMERCIAL TIRE VAN (NO NUMBER), ISSUED 1935. 1/43 SCALE.

NO. 713 LA SALLE SEDAN AND NO. 712 LA SALLE COUPE. BOTH ARE 1/43 SCALE AND 108 MM. THEY WERE ISSUED IN 1935 AND ARE MODELS OF THE 1935 LA SALLE. THE LA SALLES ARE HIGHLY DESIRABLE TO COLLECTORS.

NO. 716 DOODLEBUG, 102 MM LONG. PATTERNED AFTER A BRIGGS PROTO-TYPE SEDAN. ISSUED IN 1935.

NO. 118 DE SOTO AIRFLOW, ISSUED IN 1935. 76 MM.

NO. 112 FORD COUPE AND NO. 111 FORD SEDAN, REP-RESENTING 1935 FORDS, IS-SUED IN 1935. BOTH 76 MM.

the body casting, including open fenders and inner axle pillars, and a separate piece much like that of the Grahams, with grille, headlights and front bumper riveted to the body in the usual way. The Ford Wrecker, unlike its Graham counterpart, has its towing hook cast integrally with the crane boom. The Fords lack rear bumpers entirely. They ran on rubber tires and metal hubs smaller than those of the Grahams and Macks. In this form the Fords were produced only in 1935, after which their construction and wheels were changed.

Two new Mack trucks appeared in 1935; one was the no. 810 Railway Express Truck, issued for two years in three-piece form with separate chassis, cab and rear-body castings. The first two castings are identical to those of the other Macks; the third is an open-topped box with a plain front, solid side panels carrying decals, and rear bars. The box was riveted to the chassis and held the back of the cab in place. The truck was painted dark green and issued with decals including the Railway Express Agency name and emblems and, in the center, a large advertisement for Wrigley's Spearmint chewing gum. The bright, colorful decals made the truck particularly eye-catching, and it has enjoyed a popularity matched by few of the other Macks.

In 1936 this model, like most other Macks, was revised to consist of a single chassis/cab casting to which the rear box was riveted as before. A horizontal bar was added to the box's rear stakes to make them sturdier. The length of the model remained 103 mm, the color remained green, and the number of wheels and tires remained four, for this truck never had dual rear wheels. It stayed in production through 1941.

The no. 198 Mack Auto Transport, 277 mm long, is an updating of the earlier types, with the usual cab unit and a tinplate semi-trailer revised to hold three small Fords: two Sedans and a Coupe. In 1936 the second-type Mack cab replaced the first, and the hitching post was lowered; in this form the model was produced through 1941.

Here at last the long line of 1935 Tootsietoy issues comes to an end. It was an eventful year, all the more so after the doldrums of 1934, but it could not quite equal the splendor and importance of 1933. It marked the end of an era, for the LaSalles and Doodlebug were the last models of their kind that the firm produced, and, from 1936 on, the policy of making "toys for doodling" prevailed.

In 1936 the new small series was enlarged and modified. The Fords reappeared as single castings including a revised radiator grille, headlights and a full front bumper. The models now ran on small white rubber wheels. For a short time the grilles were painted silver, and the Convertible Coupe and Sedan were issued with their usual tan tops; later the Convertibles were deleted and each model was painted a single color, grille and all.

Despite the eventual deletion of no. 114 and no. 115, the series was growing, for three models were added in 1936. The no. 116 Ford Roadster is a single casting, 78 mm long, with an open interior that includes a detailed seat, folded convertible top, featureless floor and dash with no steering wheel. The problem of making a sturdy windshield was solved by casting it in folded position on the hood. The body was painted a basic color, with the interior brown and the grille silver at first; later the entire car appeared in a single color.

Two small trucks joined the series in the same year. The no. 120 Oil Tank Truck is sometimes called a Ford but more closely resembles a Federal truck, a much larger vehicle than the Fords; incongruously, the 74 mm model is actually smaller than the Ford models. This rugged cab-over-engine tanker would have made a much better model in a larger scale, but the selling price of the series controlled the production cost and limited the size. Still it is an impressive little model of the most modern-looking truck the firm had portrayed up to that time.

Its companion is the no. 121 Ford Pickup Truck, also a 74 mm single casting with white rubber wheels. It features a V-shaped grille, enclosed cab, and open rear box with sides that flare out from the cab. Like the tanker, this truck was painted a basic color, with silver grille at first. Both trucks were produced through 1939.

NO. 1043 CAMPING TRAILER SET, COMPRISED OF A NO. 112 FORD COUPE AND AN UNNUMBERED CAMPING TRAILER SOLD ONLY IN THE SET. THE SET WAS ISSUED IN 1937.

NO. 113 FORD WRECKER, ISSUED IN 1935. 81 MM.

NO. 810 MACK RAILWAY EXPRESS TRUCK, ISSUED 1935. 1/43 SCALE, 103 MM. REPRESENTS 1932 AC BULLDOG.

NO. 198 MACK AUTO TRANSPORT WITH NO. 111 FORD SEDAN, NO. 112 FORD COUPE AND NO. 113 FORD WRECKER. THE CARS REPRESENT 1934-MODEL FORDS. THE MACK IS A 1932 AC, 277 MM, 1/43 SCALE AND WAS ISSUED IN 1935.

NO. 116 FORD ROADSTER, 1936 ISSUE. 78 MM.

Another 1936 issue was the firm's first military aircraft, the no. 119 U.S. Army Plane, a single casting 70 mm long with 101 mm wingspan. The plane has a single nine-cylinder radial engine with a separate cast propeller, a projecting cockpit frame, and the usual stabilizers and tailfin, with a cast-in skid below. Circled star rondels and U.S. ARMY lettering are cast into the wings. Two struts hold the axle with its two white rubber wheels. The model was made until the war.

From 1936 through 1941 the firm produced a Midget Assortment of very small one-piece miniatures often referred to by collectors as Cracker Jacks, suggesting a link between the Dowst firm and its old associates in the confectionery business. The 1941 catalogue shows a boxed set of twelve pieces, each a single casting including the non-moving wheels. At that time the twelve were a Doodlebug, bus, wrecker, camelback van, speed record car (the only version of the Bluebird ever painted blue), fire engine, Zephyr railcar, battleship, submarine and one-, two- and four-engine planes. Also in existence, and perhaps included in the boxed set at times, are a stake truck, ambulance, Overland Bus (the one in the 1941 set is a more modern type), cannon, tank, two-engine bomber plane and a very small ocean liner, and there may well be others. Some of them were indeed used as 'surprises' in boxes of Cracker Jacks, and some may have been used as playing pieces for games.

Though the trend toward smaller, simpler and cheaper Tootsietoys was evident, 1936 also brought the first of what was then called the Jumbo and later the Torpedo series. All the Jumbos are single castings, 146 to 149 mm long, and their original two-tone paint or silver trim later gave way to solid colors.

The first of them is the no. 1016 Roadster, which looks enough like a real Auburn boat-tail roadster to be called that by collectors. The grille with its V-shaped bars, the long hood with four projections on the left that may represent exhaust pipes, and the long tapering tail resemble those features of the 1935-36 Auburn Speedster, but other details do not. The cab is featureless except for seat detail, the windshield is a solid part of the casting with no opening, and the headlights and taillights are set into the fenders in a very un-Auburnlike manner. Still the model looks more like a real car than do most of the Jumbos. Like the others, it has used a variety of wheels. The prewar issues had either large metal hubs and rubber tires (bigger than the Graham type) or large white rubber tires with chromed hubcaps held in place by two pointed tabs sticking into the rubber. The very last prewar type had wooden wheels, and when the models were reissued after the war they had black rubber wheels. At first, full axles were used, but these gave way to half-axles driven into metal sleeves which, unlike those of the Bild-a-Car Grahams, were not meant to allow dismantling. The Roadster's axles are carried on four tabs descending from the body. The model is usually found in a single color, often yellow, though early issues have silver grille and bumpers and a contrasting-color dashboard, floor and seat.

The next two members do not share the moderately real look of the Roadster. The no. 1017 Coupe is a crudely modernistic car vaguely like a Pierce-Arrow Silver Arrow of the mid-thirties. Its rear fenders include full skirts with axle holes; the front fenders were open at first, with axle pillars inside, but later they were made with very unreal partial skirts just big enough to provide axle holes.

The no. 1018 Sedan looks no more realistic than the Coupe. Its sleek four-door body vaguely resembles a Hupmobile, but its hood and grille are too crude and ugly to resemble any real car. The axles were carried in the same ways as those of the Coupe, and both models appeared first with two-tone paint and/or silver trim, and later in a single color.

Realism returned in the no. 1019 Pickup Truck, which bears some resemblance to the small no. 121 Ford but more to a real International truck. Its grille is basically V-shaped but with a bit of concavity, its hood and cab are realistic, and its sides, like those of the small Ford, flare out before running back to the tailboard. The fenders are open and the axles are held by pillars at the front and smaller tabs at the rear. The Pickup first appeared with cab,

FORD ROADSTER FIRE
CHIEF CAR, SOLD ONLY IN
SETS, VERY RARE.

NO. 120 OIL TANK TRUCK.
SOMETIMES CALLED A FORD
BUT MORE CLOSELY RESEM-
BLES A FEDERAL. ISSUED IN
1936, 74 MM.

NO. 121 FORD PICKUP
TRUCK, ISSUED 1936. 74 MM.

NO. 119 U.S. ARMY PLANE. 70
MM LONG WITH 101 MM
WINGSPAN. ISSUED IN 1936.

MIDGET ASSORTMENT, ONE-
INCH MODELS.

rear bed, grille and front bumper in silver and the rest in one color; later the entire truck was painted a single color.

These four models, plus two later additions, were renamed the Torpedo series in 1940. They were reissued after the war, always with one-color paint and black rubber wheels on sleeved half-axles. Their more-or-less unreal styling shows that the firm's tradition of making models of real vehicles was all but dead.

The no. 1026 Cross Country Bus was added to the Jumbo series in 1937. Its number was soon changed to 1045 for reasons that escape us. At 150 mm it is the longest model in the series, as it deserves to be. Its appearance, though stylized and modernistic, is fairly realistic. The rear fenders are fully skirted, while the originally open front fenders were later given partial skirts and the axle pillars eliminated. The GREYHOUND name is cast on the middle of each side. A later version, made for a boxed set, bore TRANS-AMERICA lettering instead and is extremely rare. At first the bus was equipped with a sheet-metal base, including some chassis detail; four tabs wrapped around the bumpers to hold it on. This type can be found with either large metal hubs and rubber tires or with rubber wheels and chromed hubcaps. The hubs and tires also appear on a later prewar version without a base, and wooden wheels were also used just before the war. Postwar versions have black rubber wheels. At first the model had two-tone paint, usually blue and silver, the latter used for grille, fenders and an area around the cast-in name. Later versions were painted a single color, usually some shade of blue.

The last Jumbo, the no. 1027 Wrecker, was also issued in 1937. Somewhat realistic, it resembles a Chevrolet, but is even more stylized than the bus. The crane boom is particularly unreal; it ends in a sturdy towing hook attached to the back edge of the body by a short bar. Wheel, axle and paint variations are as on the other Jumbo models. All six Jumbos were sold to dealers in the no. 1025 Torpedo assortment (assortments were boxed lots out of which retailers sold the pieces individually), and were used in several sets as well. The no. 5210 Truck Set of 1936-38, which was renamed the Commercial Set from 1939 through 1941, included a variety of models that changed from year to year. In 1941 it was composed of the Torpedo Pickup and Wrecker, two of the large 1938 tank trucks, the 1940 pickup truck and station wagon, a large hook and ladder truck, two small trucks and the Waco Navy Bomber of 1937, the last item referred to as "the type that carry the Nation's air-mail and air express." The station wagons, of which two were included, were called "cars that can be 'loaded' with freight," and no attempt was made to justify the ladder truck. The no. 750 Jumbo Set included the three cars and the red and silver Trans-America Bus (its only use), and carried on the first name of the series to 1941.

In 1937 the Doodlebug was revised into the no. 6015 Lincoln Zephyr. The front and rear castings were eliminated and the model was made into a single casting, 104 mm long, with a sleek pointed hood, two grille panels, and a single large spotlight at the rear to replace the taillights in the fenders. In this form the Zephyr was available through 1939. A variation, the no. 6016 Wrecker, lasted only through 1938. It differed from the Zephyr only in having a large boom and hook in place of the rear spotlight. It looked silly, and as if a Lincoln turned into a wrecker were not bad enough, this model, along with the regular Zephyr, was issued for a time with an Oriental windup motor of poor quality. The motor was mounted on internal rivets and key-wound through a hole in the left rear door. These motors often broke down, and as soon as the supply of them was used up these versions were deleted.

The Roamer Trailer, no. 1044, was issued in 1937 and was meant to be pulled by a La Salle at first, but a towing loop could not be added to the LaSalle so a trailer hitch was added to the Zephyr instead. The Roamer is 120 mm long and consists of a main body casting, a diecast sliding door and a sheet-metal base. The body is that of a boxy house trailer with three curtained windows on each side, a plain one at the rear, and the sliding door on the right, moving on rails inside the body. Two ventilator pipes and two hatches are on the roof,

MIDGET ASSORTMENT, ONE-INCH MODELS.

NO. 1016 JUMBO/TORPEDO ROADSTER. THE JUMBO/TORPEDO CAR MODELS WERE ISSUED IN 1936 AND VARIED IN LENGTH FROM 146–149 MM. THIS ONE IS CALLED AN AUBURN BY COLLECTORS. REISSUED POSTWAR SIX-INCH.

NO. 1017 JUMBO/TORPEDO COUPE. REISSUED POSTWAR SIX-INCH.

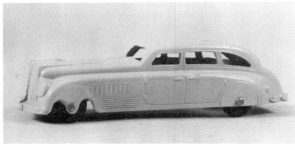

NO. 1018 JUMBO/TORPEDO SEDAN. REISSUED POSTWAR SIX-INCH.

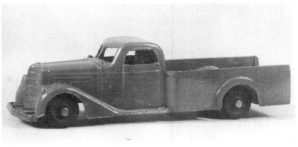

NO. 1019 JUMBO/TORPEDO PICKUP TRUCK. BEARS SOME RESEMBLANCE TO AN INTERNATIONAL TRUCK. REISSUED POSTWAR SIX-INCH.

and the left side bears TOOTSIETOY ROAMER lettering. A tongue hooks to the car that pulls the trailer, and a heavy ridge around the bottom of the body is gripped by six tabs that hold the base on, while two other tabs provide axle holes. Metal hubs with rubber tires are used. The model was painted a solid color and remained in production as long as the Zephyr was there to pull it.

Since 1934 there had not been a single fire truck in the Tootsietoy line. The gap was filled in 1937 with three trucks that resemble 1937 Macks. The no. 1040 Hook and Ladder is the longest, being 139 mm long with its three ladders, though the truck without them is roughly the same size as the other two. The single casting portrays a plain, simple truck with open cab, ladder racks and no unnecessary details. The three ladders are made to interlock, and one can be set in two holes on the rear deck. To the model was added a diecast driver, who plugs into a rivet hole in his seat much like the driver of the old no. 23 Racer. He wears a fireman's hat and coat and holds a steering wheel. In its prewar form this truck, with its two companions, used white rubber tires on metal hubs, with the axles held by pillars or tabs, and was painted red with silver trim. All three were reissued after the war with various changes; the ladder truck alone was not modified before the war.

The no. 1041 Hose Car, 115 mm long, is the most striking of the three fire trucks. In front of its hood a large pump stands between the bumper mountings. The open driver's seat and its occupant are much like those of the ladder truck. Behind the seat is a large block of hose, and a swiveling water cannon is mounted on the rear deck. In 1938 a step was added to the tailboard, with a hole in it to take a new casting, that of a standing fireman whose hands nearly touch the butt of the water gun when it faces forward. Like the ladder truck it was painted red with silver trim; the two men were blue or sometimes gold.

Following the precedent set by the small 1931 Mack, the firm called no. 1042 an Insurance Patrol, though it is actually a fire pumper of another kind than the Hose Car. Measuring 109 mm, it looks rather like the ladder truck in general, but has some features all its own. Its first version has a narrow rear deck around a similarly narrow well. A year or two later this well was eliminated, and the new deck was fitted with two bars to hold a ladder and two holes to stand it in. A standing fireman like that on the Hose Car was added at the rear, along with a step to which he was riveted. The truck was painted red, with much more silver trim on the first than on the second type.

In these forms the three fire trucks remained in production until the war. They were offered to dealers in the no. 1050 Fire Department Assortment and were used in several sets, while both no. 1042 versions were adapted for military use.

A small Camping Trailer was issued in 1937 and sold along with one of the small Ford Sedans or Coupes as set no. 1043. The 80 mm trailer, never issued alone, is a single casting running on two small rubber wheels and made with a long towbar with a U-shaped hook at its end. Since the Fords had no rear bumpers, the towbar passed under the car and hooked onto the rear axle. It could also hook onto the Airflow but was never sold with it. The trailer was painted a solid color, usually red or blue, to match the Ford it was sold with. The set was produced through 1941.

Finally, 1937 brought one more addition to the small series itself, the no. 123 Light Delivery Truck, often called a Ford but apparently modeled after a Dodge. It is popularly known as the Camelback Van on account of its shape, or the Special Delivery Van because of the lettering on its side panels. It was not meant to be a mail truck, but the delivery van of a department store, and in addition to the regular version others were prepared with names of stores. The truck is a single casting, 77 mm long, with the usual small rubber wheels. The hump formed where the rear body meets the cab gives the truck its popular camelback name.

The Special Delivery version was painted a single color, often a dull dusty blue but sometimes a striking silver. With one exception the types prepared for specific stores had

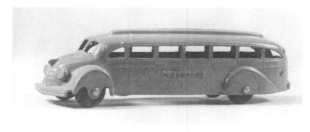

NO. 1045 JUMBO/TORPEDO CROSS COUNTRY BUS, FIRST ISSUED IN 1937 AS NO. 1026 BUT NUMBER WAS SOON CHANGED FOR UNKNOWN REASONS. 150 MM. REISSUED POSTWAR SIX-INCH.

NO. 1027 JUMBO/TORPEDO WRECKER, ISSUED 1937. 150 MM. RESEMBLES A CHEVROLET. REISSUED POSTWAR SIX-INCH.

NO. 6015 LINCOLN ZEPHYR. A REVISED VERSION OF THE DOODLEBUG, THE ZEPHYR WAS ISSUED IN 1937. IT IS 1/43 SCALE AND 104 MM.

NO. 6016 LINCOLN ZEPHYR WRECKER, ISSUED IN 1937. 1/43 SCALE, 104 MM.

NO. 1044 ROAMER TRAILER, ISSUED IN 1937. 1/43 SCALE, 120 MM.

plain side panels to which name decals were applied. The Lewis's truck, made for a British firm, is dark green; the McLean's bright blue; the Wieboldt's green; and the Miller & Rhoads black. A Shepard's van was also made, using lithographed inserts instead of decals, and there may have been other special issues as well. Less is actually known about these store-name vans than about the earlier Federals.

Several models were added to the Tootsietoy air fleet in 1937. Perhaps the most impressive is the no. 718 Waco Bomber, a single-engine blue-and-silver biplane. It consists of two castings: one comprising the upper wing, tail and top of the fuselage; the other including the bottom of the fuselage, the shorter lower wing and the landing gear. Two rubber wheels and a diecast propeller complete the model. The upper wing has circled star rondels and U.S. NAVY lettering. It remained in production until the war.

The bulbous no. 719 Crusader Plane did not last as long. Like the Waco, it is made of two castings; the larger one comprises the wings, twin fuselage booms, connecting tail and the lower part of a large central cabin. The smaller second casting forms the top of the cabin. Each fuselage boom has an engine with propeller, plus a wheel housing underneath. The two castings were painted in contrasting colors. This odd-looking plane must have been unpopular; it was withdrawn before 1941.

Another 1937 plane was the no. 125 Lockheed Electra which, like the Waco, was produced until the war. It is a conventional twin-engine airliner, much smaller than the other planes, with a length of 67 mm and a wingspan of 100 mm. A single casting meant to sell with the other low-priced items, it has considerably less detail than the larger planes, but it still manages to look sleek, modern and handsome, though its two rubber wheels and two three-bladed propellers are too big for it.

The *Los Angeles* Dirigible, no. 1030, forms a link of sorts between these more or less typical aircraft and the fantastic spacecraft issued in the same year. Its two castings form the left and right sides of its sleek ribbed body; they are joined internally and make a model 130 mm long. The dirigible's good looks, alas, are spoiled by two large pairs of tabs atop it that hold two pulleys (actually diecast wheel hubs) under which a string can be passed. The model was in fact sold with a long string, and one could send it sailing across the playroom by raising one end of the string.

The same arrangement was used a bit less obtrusively on the three Buck Rogers Rocket Ships of the same year. Like the earlier Funnies series, this set, no. 5460, was a sales failure and was withdrawn along with the *Los Angeles* at the end of 1938. One of the ships, the Battlecruiser, bearing number TSDM 3030 along with its name and painted yellow and red, looks vaguely like a submarine out of water. Somewhat similar but fatter is the white and blue Venus Duo-Destroyer, numbered MK 24L, and featuring a small cigar-shaped cabin on top to hold the two pulleys, which are housed in small fins on the Battlecruiser. Quite unlike these is the Flash Blast Attack Ship, painted white and red and numbered TS 310 Z. Despite its awesome name it looks like two gigantic golf balls attached to each other by four booms, the top boom including a small cabin and a pair of wings that hold the pulleys. The other two ships look at least vaguely like spacecraft, but the Flash Blast—well, one just doesn't expect to see golf balls in outer space.

The following year, 1938, brought only one unusual aircraft, the no. 720 Fly-n-Gyro. It looks much like the Autogyro with a few major differences: its wings do not tilt upward at their tips, but its rotors tilt up from their mountings, and it includes two pulleys and can be strung on a string. Between the pulleys the string can be wound around the rotor shaft to make the blades turn as the craft glides through the air. As for more mundane details, the model is a single casting with a three-bladed propeller and two rubber wheels. The pulley housings prevent it from having a cockpit. It was withdrawn before 1941.

The big event of 1938 was the production of a set of four oil tankers, models of Reo trucks though not identified as such. Each bears the name of a different brand of petroleum

NO. 1040 HOOK AND LAD-
DER TRUCK, A 1937 MACK,
ISSUED IN 1937. 1/43 SCALE,
139 MM. REISSUED POST-
WAR FOUR-INCH.

NO. 1041 HOSE CAR, A 1937
MACK, ISSUED IN 1937. 1/43
SCALE, 115 MM. REISSUED
POSTWAR FOUR-INCH.

NO. 1042 INSURANCE PA-
TROL, A 1937 MACK FIRE
PUMPER, ISSUED IN 1937.
1/43 SCALE, 109 MM. RE-
ISSUED POSTWAR FOUR-
INCH.

NO. 1042 INSURANCE PA-
TROL, SECOND TYPE.

NO. 123 LIGHT DELIVERY
TRUCK—PROMOTIONAL VER-
SION: SHEPARD. ISSUED IN
1937, 77 MM. APPARENTLY
MODELED AFTER 1936
DODGE.

products on its signboards, but aside from these names and the colors of the models, the four are identical. The front of the truck forms a wide vee, with the grille projecting a bit from the rest of the cab-over-engine body. The cab doors are directly over the front fenders, and the greater part of the truck's length is taken up by the five-section tank with a signboard along each side and a huge filler cap atop the middle section. All four fenders have skirts with axle holes; the large metal hubs with rubber tires are mounted inside the body. The single casting is 149 mm long. No. 1006 bears the Standard name and is painted red with silver fenders, grille, bumpers, lights and lettering. The no. 1007 Sinclair truck is green with black lettering and silver tank and trim. The no. 1008 Texaco type is red with black lettering and silver tank and trim, while the no. 1009 Shell truck is yellow with red trim, lettering and fenders. In addition to the name, its signboards have a Shell emblem at each end. The four tankers were sold to dealers in the no. 1005 Oil Truck Assortment, and some were used in sets. They were produced until the war and probably reissued afterward, though another set of four tankers soon replaced them.

Since war was obviously coming, a new military vehicle was made in 1938, the no. 4635 Armored Car. It is a single casting, 100 mm long, produced until the war with either large rubber tires on metal hubs or white rubber wheels with chromed hubcaps, and reissued afterward with plain rubber wheels. The car's body is grim and angular, with U.S. ARMY lettering on the sides and a raised turret from whose slitlike gun ports two machine guns protrude. Two blobs on the guns straddled the window sills, but they came out easily and were later eliminated. At first the model was painted a solid gray, bronze or khaki; later it appeared with green and tan camouflage paint.

Two sets first offered in 1938 combined models already in production for at least a year. The no. 180 Roamer Set held the Lincoln Zephyr with modified rear bumper and the Roamer Trailer. The set went out of production along with its components at the end of 1939. The other, which was produced through 1941, is the no. 411 Fire Department Set, with the three 1937 fire trucks, four ladders, a fire badge and a chief's car. At first a red Ford Coupe was used; in 1939 it was replaced by a red Ford Roadster equipped like the truck with a fireman driver, and so it remained until it was withdrawn.

In 1939 both varieties of the no. 1042 fire truck were put to military use as the no. 4634 Army Supply Truck. A rounded tinplate top, like that of a Conestoga wagon, completely covers the rear body and is held on by tabs through slits in the truck. Otherwise the vehicle is unchanged except for its khaki paint; the driver, in fact, still wears his fireman's helmet! Since both versions of no. 1042 were used, we know that the first version was not withdrawn when the second was introduced. The Supply Truck remained in production until the war.

Another 1939 model was produced in both civilian and (later) military form: the Super Mainliner, a model of the Douglas DC-4, which seems to have been its catalogue number in civilian colors. It is made of two castings, the upper one providing the top of the fuselage and the central tail fin; the lower piece consists of everything else, including the stabilizers with small fins at their ends. The model is 95 mm long with a wingspan of 132 mm, has four three-bladed propellers and three small metal wheels. The wings are lettered UNITED and NC 20100. The no. 722 Transport Plane was introduced in 1941 as a military version, and the civilian Mainliner was dropped. Camouflage colors replaced the original silver, and circled star rondels appeared on the wings in place of the earlier lettering.

The other new issues of 1939 were railroad locomotives and freight cars. Two locomotives were made, the no. 1076 Santa Fe and no. 1086 Pennsylvania, both 4-6-2 in terms of cast-in wheels but actually running on four rubber wheels inside the casting, which included the tender as well as the engine. The two models differ only in the railroad names on the sides of the tenders.

The two engines were accompanied by nine freight cars, each 130 mm long except the

NO. 123 LIGHT DELIVERY
TRUCKS—PROMOTIONAL:
WIEBOLDT'S AND LEWIS'S.

NO. 123 LIGHT DELIVERY
TRUCKS: LEWIS'S AND STAN-
DARD ISSUE SPECIAL DE-
LIVERY.

NO. 123 LIGHT DELIVERY
TRUCKS—PROMOTIONAL:
MILLER & RHOADS AND
MCLEAN'S.

NO. 125 LOCKHEED ELEC-
TRA, ISSUED IN 1937. 67 MM
LONG, WITH A WINGSPAN OF
100 MM.

NO. 1030 DIRIGIBLE "LOS
ANGELES," ISSUED IN 1937.
130 MM.

shorter caboose. They are as follows:

> 1087 Wrecking Crane, a silver flatcar with red or green swiveling cabin and long crane boom.
> 1088 Refrigerator Car, a red and yellow single casting with Armour's advertising.
> 1089 Box Car, red and white, with Southern Fruit Growers' Express logo.
> 1090 Coal Car, a gondola, a single casting including the top of its load, copper and black when carrying coal, green and tan with sand.
> 1091 Stock Car, a single casting, yellow and brown or brown and orange, with Pioneer Stock Shippers logo.
> 1092 Log Car, a silver flatcar with a load of dowels glued together.
> 1093 Milk Tank Car, a single-casting tanker, white and red, in Borden's livery.
> 1094 Oil Tank Car, practically identical, red and silver, in Sinclair livery.
> 1095 Caboose, 80 mm long, the older caboose with rubber wheels but otherwise unchanged.

The two tank cars were at first separate castings; later the cast-in names were eliminated and a single casting was produced, with a plain name board to which adhesive paper labels could be applied. The cars hitched together by means of front hooks and rear loops. They were joined by a series of passenger cars. Some, if not all, were reissued after the war.

Before we leave 1939 it must be noted that various Tootsietoys appeared around that time with plated finish in the Coppertoys and Silvertoys Sets; so one may find some models of this era with copper or silver finish as well as in their usual colors.

In 1940 a new set of ten small models took the place of the Ford series, and two of its members also appeared in larger form. One of the latter is the no. 1010 Wrigley Truck, a stylized, snub-nosed pickup vaguely like a GMC truck. The 114 mm single casting has just enough nose to avoid being called cab-over-engine, a notch in the body just behind the cab, and then a sort of camel's-hump cabinet in front of the open rear body. A large slot at each end of the bed suggests that the use of a rear cover or load might have been planned. The rear sides carry Wrigley's Spearmint decals different from those of the Railway Express truck. This model was originally painted in a basic color, usually yellow, green or blue, with silver trim, and ran on white rubber wheels with chrome hubcaps. After the war it was reissued with black rubber wheels and without decals or silver trim.

Its companion, the no. 1046 Station Wagon, is a single casting 113 mm long. Less stylized than the pickup, it is quite realistic and probably represents a 1938 Ford wagon. The main part of the body is detailed to look like wood, and in prewar form this was painted tan and the rest of the car green, blue or red with silver trim. It ran on white rubber wheels with hubcaps. The postwar reissue was painted a single color and had black rubber wheels.

The ten small models usually known as the 230 series replaced almost all of the earlier Fords. First came the no. 230 Sedan, 83 mm long, like all its kin a single casting with small white (or, after the war, black) rubber wheels. It resembles the 1939 LaSalle limousine and has at times been offered for Tootsietoy LaSalle prices by not overly honest folk. It was painted a basic color, often red or green, and in prewar form it had silver trim. The same is true of almost every model in the 230 series.

No. 231 is a Coupe, 79 mm long, somewhat like a 1939 Chevrolet and usually painted green. Then came two open cars, the no. 232 Touring Car, a four-seat convertible resembling a Buick, and the no. 233 Roadster, a boat-tailed two-seater somewhat like a 1939 Ford. Both have detailed seats, featureless dashboards, and low solid windshields. The 75 mm Touring Car was usually painted red or blue, the 80 mm Roadster blue.

The no. 234 Box Truck is a small version of the Wrigley pickup, 79 mm long, a bit slimmer than the big one, and usually painted yellow. The no. 235 Oil Truck replaced but could not equal the rugged good looks of the little Federal tanker. Its 79 mm body is quite plain and dull, though various casting changes were made to it, probably after the war. The

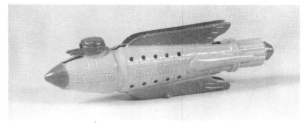

BUCK ROGERS ROCKET SHIP
BATTLECRUISER, FROM THE
NO. 5460 BUCK ROGERS
ROCKET SHIP SET THAT WAS
ISSUED IN 1937.

BUCK ROGERS BATTLE-
CRUISER.

BUCK ROGERS VENUS DUO-
DESTROYER.

BUCK ROGERS VENUS DUO-
DESTROYER.

BUCK ROGERS FLASH BLAST
ATTACK SHIP.

prewar version appeared with silver tank and trim and the rest of the truck usually blue or red.

Next came three fire trucks that resembled Macks but not the three big Mack fire engines. No. 236 is a Hook and Ladder Truck with open cab, cast-in driver and ladders, and a big siren on the hood just in front of the solid windshield. No. 237 was called an Insurance Patrol but is a pumper with hose reel, couplings and searchlight to the rear and a large bell on the hood. Like the Hook and Ladder, it has an open cab with cast-in driver and solid windshield. So does the no. 238 Hose Car, which like its larger counterpart features a water cannon, in this case cast integrally with the rest of the truck. It has a siren on its hood, instead of a bell. All three trucks were painted red with silver trim before the war.

The series ends with the no. 239 Station Wagon, a 76 mm version of no. 1046. It was originally painted in two colors to represent the wood and metal parts of its body, with silver trim as well, and ran on white rubber wheels. Like its fellows, it was reissued after the war with black wheels, and painted a single color, in this case orange.

All ten models were included in the no. 5150 Motor Set, while the three fire trucks, the small Federal tanker and two ladders made up the no. 184 Fire Department Set. The no. 550 Fire Department Assortment offered retailers just the three fire trucks, while the no. 525 Rol-Ezy Assortment contained the other seven plus the no. 113 Ford Wrecker. Since this model remained in production, we wonder why the Federal Tanker was replaced by no. 235, yet retained for the fire set. In any case, the 230 series livened up 1940 and must have sold very well, for their prewar forms are almost as common as the postwar reissues.

Tootsietoy production in 1941 showed the impact of the war, even though the United States had not yet entered it. Some models appeared with wooden wheels as rubber grew scarce, and several items shown in the 1941 catalogue only got as far as the pilot-model stage. Others went into production but were made, or at least sold, only in small quantities. Perhaps the rarest is the no. 187 Auto Carrier, 216 mm long, consisting of a one-piece Mack cab unit (its last use) with an offset hitching pin and a sheet metal two-wheel trailer carrying three 230 series cars at an angle. This model is so rare that collectors once suspected that it had never been issued. It was, though, with a red cab and yellow trailer.

Even the learned Mr. Lee once doubted the existence of the no. 1011 Farm Tractor, but since then several red and silver specimens have come to light. The two colors are those of the model's separate body and chassis castings, which are held together by two rivets through tabs near the front, and by the driver's arms and a bar between them that hook over the steering wheel. The wheels are of black rubber, the front ones small and plain, the rear pair identical to those used on the Long Range Cannon. This model is almost but not quite as rare as the no. 187 Auto Carrier or the Trans-America Bus that appeared in 1941 in the no. 750 Jumbo Set.

Four models advertised in 1941 never got into production and exist at the factory as unfinished pilot models. These are the no. 260 Yellow Cab, no. 261 Checker Cab, no. 262 Fire Engine and no. 263 Hook and Ladder Truck, all meant to be about 185 mm long. The two taxis appear to be the same car, probably meant to be distinguished by paint or lettering, but the two fire trucks are quite different, though both have open cabs with drivers.

The remaining new issues were aircraft. No. 721 is the Curtis P-40 Pursuit Plane, a single casting representing a typical World War II fighter with closed cockpit, single propeller and two rubber wheels mounted on an axle but housed in skirts. Both the 1941 catalogue and Mr. Lee spell the name 'Curtis,' despite the fact that aviation pioneer Glenn Curtiss, founder of the firm that later became Curtiss-Wright, did not. The no. 722 Transport Plane, a modified DC-4 Mainliner in camouflage paint, has already been noted, and it seems to have been followed just before production ended by a single-engine military transport plane that had a bulbous fuselage with a massive engine cowling at the nose. It was not a beautiful model, but its short life span has made it a rare one.

NO. 1007 SINCLAIR OIL TANKER, AND NO. 1006 STANDARD OIL TANKER. ISSUED IN 1938, 149 MM, THE OIL TANKERS ARE MODELS OF REO TRUCKS BUT NOT IDENTIFIED AS SUCH BY THE COMPANY. REISSUED POSTWAR SIX-INCH.

NO. 1008 TEXACO OIL TANKER, AND NO. 1009 SHELL OIL TANKER. REISSUED POSTWAR SIX-INCH.

NO. 4635 ARMORED CAR, ISSUED IN 1938. 100 MM. REISSUED POSTWAR FOUR-INCH

NO. 4634 ARMY SUPPLY TRUCK. A 1/43 SCALE MACK TRUCK, ISSUED IN 1939. 109 MM. REISSUED POSTWAR FOUR-INCH.

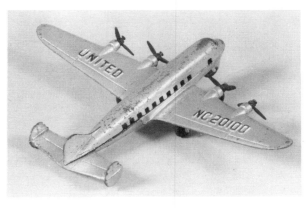

SUPER MAINLINER. CIVILIAN VERSION OF THIS DOUGLAS DC-4 MODEL USED DC-4 AS THE CATALOGUE NUMBER. ISSUED IN 1939, THE LENGTH IS 95 MM AND THE WINGSPAN IS 132 MM.

The no. 6100 Aeroplane Set included two Wings seaplanes, an Aero-Dawn, two Waco Bombers, two Army Planes, a Curtis, two Electras, a DC-2 and an Army Transport. Since some of these planes were issued in 1941, it is possible that the set existed previously with a different selection of models.

Many other sets and assortments are shown in the 1941 catalogue, and they deserve mention though we cannot say just when they were issued. The no. 5000 Motor Set includes a mixed bag of vehicles: two Army Planes, two Electras, the big Bluebird, the Ford Wrecker and fourteen 230 series items: three Coupes, two Roadsters, two Station Wagons and one each of the others. Three different Playtime Sets were available: no. 5050, with seven 230 series cars and trucks, the Ford Wrecker, Army Plane and Electra; the completely different no. 5100 with the whole Torpedo series, the bigger ladder and hose trucks, the Waco Bomber and Mainliner; and the small no. 199 with the 230 series Sedan, Coupe, Roadster and Tanker and the Army Plane.

Several military sets were offered, including the no. 650 Army Set that includes the Armored Car, Supply Truck, Cannon, Waco Navy Bomber (in an army set?) and nine soldiers; and the larger no. 5220 of the same name, with the Tank, Armored Car, the two Mack Army trucks, the Graham Army Ambulance (with black rubber wheels), Supply Truck, two Cannons, two Army Planes, two miniature bombers and, once again, the Waco. Dealers were offered the no. 4625 Military Assortment of Tank, Armored Car, Supply Truck, Cannon, the two Macks and the Ambulance. Finally, a Land Defense Set, no. 1404, offered ten soldiers mounted on a cardboard sheet with no vehicles.

A similar Air Defense Set, no. 1407, was composed of ten miniature bombers in varying colors. The no. 189 Air Raiders Set included the Waco, Mainliner, Electra, DC-2, Curtis and Army Plane. Two Aeroplane Assortments were available, no. 575 with the smaller planes that sold for five cents each, and no. 1075 with the larger ten-cent items.

Ten different ships, most of them warlike, were issued in or shortly before 1941, and were divided into two dealer lots. The ten-cent Boat Assortment, no. 1081, included the six larger types: no. 1034 Battleship, no. 1035 Cruiser, no. 1036 Aeroplane Carrier, no. 1037 Transport, no. 1038 Freighter and no. 1039 Tanker. The four smaller craft were in the no. 135 five-cent Boat Assortment: no. 127 Destroyer, no. 128 Submarine, no. 129 Tender and, strikingly out of place among the others, no. 130 Yacht. The ships were basically single castings, though some had additional pieces such as guns or airplanes; they ran on small diecast pairs of wheels inside their hulls. The ships were painted in either camouflage colors or combinations of black, gray, white and red.

Among the sets of ships were the no. 5700 Navy Fleet of three Battleships, three Cruisers and two each of the Destroyer, Submarine and Carrier; the no. 5750 Navy Set of Submarine, Destroyer, Battleship, Cruiser, Carrier and Transport; the no. 5900 Convoy Set of four Destroyers, two Transports, two Tenders, a Cruiser, a Tanker and three Freighters; and the no. 179 Mosquito Fleet of two Submarines, two Destroyers and a Tender. Two other sets were made of miniature ships mounted on cards: no. 1405 Fleet with nine battleships in different colors and with different names, and no. 1408 Naval Defense with six battleships and eight even smaller craft.

The 1939 trains were joined by three passenger cars: no. 1101 Baggage Car, no. 1102 Pullman and no. 1103 Observation Car, each about 125 mm long, with two-tone paint and small rubber wheels. They were used in two train sets: no. 5850 Passenger Limited, with the Pennsylvania engine, a Baggage Car, two Pullmans and an Observation Car; and the similar no. 5851 Santa Fe Set, with the Santa Fe locomotive and the same four cars.

The freight cars appeared in several sets: no. 5550 Freight Set, with the Pennsylvania loco, Log Car, Stock Car, Milk Tank Car and Crane; no. 5600 Freight Set with the same engine and one each of the nine freight cars; and no. 1085 Freight Assortment with the same composition as no. 5600. In addition, a completely different Fast Freight, no. 186 was pro-

A COMPLETE FREIGHT TRAIN: NO. 1086 PENNSYLVANIA LOCOMOTIVE, NO. 1094 OIL TANK CAR, NO. 1093 MILK TANK CAR, NO. 1088 REFRIGERATOR CAR, NO. 1091 STOCK CAR, NO. 1087 WRECKING CRANE, NO. 1092 LOG CAR, NO. 1089 BOX CAR, NO. 1090 COAL CAR, AND NO. 1095 CABOOSE. ALL CARS ARE 130 MM LONG, EXCEPT THE CABOOSE WHICH IS 80 MM. ISSUED IN 1939.

NO. 1010 WRIGLEY TRUCK. A 114-MM 1938 GMC OPEN VAN ISSUED IN 1940. REISSUED POSTWAR FOUR-INCH.

NO. 1046 STATION WAGON. PROBABLY REPRESENTS A 1938 FORD. 1/43 SCALE, 113 MM. ISSUED IN 1940. REISSUED POSTWAR FOUR-INCH.

NO. 230 SEDAN. RESEMBLES A 1939 LA SALLE. ISSUED IN 1940, 83 MM. REISSUED POSTWAR THREE-INCH.

NO. 231 COUPE. LOOKS SOMEWHAT LIKE A 1939 CHEVROLET MASTER DELUXE. 79 MM, ISSUED IN 1940. REISSUED POSTWAR THREE-INCH.

duced, with a short 2-6-2 locomotive, separate New York Central tender, box car with Cracker Jacks logo, Texaco tanker and caboose. These pieces, shorter and simpler than the usual freight cars, were apparently not sold separately.

So ends, to the best of our knowledge, the prewar Tootsietoy story. Toy production must have slowed down drastically as American involvement in the war increased and materials grew scarce, and on June 30, 1942, it ceased altogether, to be resumed again after the war's end. And what happened afterward is another story.

NO. 232 TOURING CAR. CALLED A 1940 BUICK ROADMASTER BY COLLECTORS. ISSUED 1940, 75 MM LONG. REISSUED POSTWAR THREE-INCH.

NO. 233 ROADSTER. COULD BE A 1939 FORD STANDARD. ISSUED 1940, 80 MM. REISSUED POSTWAR THREE-INCH.

NO. 234 BOX TRUCK. A
SMALL 1939 GMC TRUCK, 79
MM, ISSUED IN 1940.

NO. 235 OIL TRUCK, SHOWN
WITHOUT AND WITH SEALED
BEAM HEADLIGHTS. ISSUED
IN 1940, 79 MM LONG, THEY
REPRESENT 1939 AND 1940
GMC TRUCKS. REISSUED
POSTWAR THREE-INCH.

THREE FIRE TRUCKS THAT
RESEMBLE MACKS: NO. 238
HOSE CAR, NO. 237 IN-
SURANCE PATROL AND NO.
236 HOOK AND LADDER. ALL
THREE INCHES AND ISSUED
IN 1940. REISSUED POSTWAR
THREE-INCH.

NO. 239 STATION WAGON. A
1938 FORD, 76 MM AND IS-
SUED IN 1940. REISSUED
POSTWAR THREE-INCH.

NO. 187 AUTO CARRIER. HAS
A 1932 MACK AC CAB. IS-
SUED IN 1941, 1/43 SCALE,
216 MM. RARE.

NO. 1011 FARM TRACTOR, MODEL OF A MASSEY-FERGUSON, ISSUED IN 1941. CONSIDERED RARE. 1/43 SCALE, FOUR INCHES.

NO. 1034 BATTLESHIP, ISSUED ABOUT 1940.

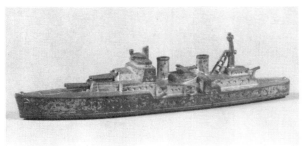

NO. 1035 CRUISER, ISSUED ABOUT 1940.

NO. 1036 AEROPLANE CARRIER, ISSUED ABOUT 1940.

NO. 1037 TRANSPORT, ISSUED ABOUT 1940.

NO. 1038 FREIGHTER, IS-
SUED ABOUT 1940.

NO. 1039 TANKER, ISSUED
ABOUT 1940.

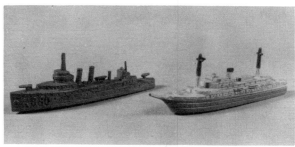

NO. 127 DESTROYER AND
NO. 130 YACHT, BOTH IS-
SUED ABOUT 1940.

NO. 1405 FLEET SET (ONE
BATTLESHIP SHOWN), NO.
129 TENDER AND NO. 128
SUBMARINE. ISSUED ABOUT
1940.

PASSENGER CARS ISSUED
IN 1940: NO. 1103 OBSERVA-
TION CAR, NO. 1101 BAG-
GAGE CAR, AND NO. 1102
PULLMAN CAR, ALONG WITH
THE 1939 NO. 1086 PENN-
SYLVANIA LOCOMOTIVE.
THE CARS ARE 125 MM
LONG.

NO. 186 FAST FREIGHT SET,
ISSUED ABOUT 1940.

1940 INTERNATIONAL K5
STAKE TRUCK, OPEN- AND
CLOSED-SIDE VERSIONS.
ALL OF THE 1940 INTER-
NATIONAL K5 TRUCKS ARE
SIX INCHES.

1940 INTERNATIONAL K5
CAR TRANSPORT.

1940 INTERNATIONAL K5
WITH GOOSENECK TRAILER
(OLDER).

1940 INTERNATIONAL K5
BOTTLE TRUCK.

1940 INTERNATIONAL K5 TOW TRUCK.

1940 INTERNATIONAL K5 DUMP TRUCK.

TRANS-AMERICA BUS (NO NUMBER). A 1937 GMC BUS ISSUED IN 1941, SIX INCHES LONG. APPEARED IN THE NO. 750 JUMBO SET. RARE.

GARAGE (UNIDENTIFIED PREWAR FROM SET).

Postwar

Tootsietoy production was resumed late in 1945. The first postwar products were reissued prewar toys. The postwar reissues can be identified by their solid black rubber wheels, replacing the white prewar tires or wheels. It was late in 1947 before any new models could be produced.

Competition from Dinky Toys, which were selling very well in the fifties, and popular demand for higher-quality products, induced the firm to issue models with lithographed baseplates beginning in 1954. Two-tone painting, which had been used on many prewar models but dropped after the war to economize on production costs, was resumed in 1954 as well, and in 1956 a tow hook was cast into the rear bumper of each car in the six-inch series so that they could pull the variety of trailers that were being introduced in gift sets. By 1957 economics caused a return to single-color models without baseplates. As a result of the many changes in production, all of the six-inch series can be found in several variations. Two-tone paint was used in the four-inch series as well, but the only four-inch car with a tow hook was the 1969 Ford LTD. Neither two-tone paint nor tow hooks ever appeared in the three-inch series. Smooth black rubber wheels were used from 1946 to 1954. These wheels, with a small hole in the middle for the axle, had a high wear rate and tended to enlarge their holes and fall off eventually. In 1954 they were replaced by patterned plastic wheels with a much lower wear rate.

The rarest car in the three-inch series is easily the 1947 Studebaker, which was sold only in a gift set and thus produced in small numbers. It was the first of the postwar models and portrayed the most exciting American car of that year. It was replaced by the Nash Metropolitan, also sold exclusively in a gift set, but this model is not quite as rare as the Studebaker. The Twin Coach Bus and the Jeepster are also more difficult to locate today than the average three-inch model, although they were abundant in their day. This is possibly due, in the case of the bus, to a public move away from mass transport at that time. The Jeepster was not a very popular car, which is probably why the model did not sell well. The most common and best-detailed three-inchers are the 1955 Ford, 1955 Chevrolet, 1957 Ford Pickup and 1954 LaFrance Fire Engine. The poorest in detail are the 1950 Plymouth and 1952 Ford, perhaps due to the increased casting cost as the Korean War caused a high demand for tool and die makers. The influx of real cars from Europe in the mid-fifties is reflected in the M.G. and Jaguar models. The smallest run of three-inchers was that of the 1960 Ford Wagon, because it was the last model added to the series and was produced for only a short time. All of the three-inchers except the Studebaker and the Twin Coach Bus can be found quite easily today, but at rapidly increasing prices. It is doubtful that any more will be found in mint condition, as they were not painted well originally.

The rarest models in the four-inch series are the 1949 Oldsmobile and the 1949 Mercury Civilian, followed by the 1941 Chrysler, 1941 International and 1955 Oldsmobile. The most readily available models are the 1954 Corvette, 1959 Pontiac and 1960 Chrysler. The lowest production was that of the 1969 Ford LTD. This issue was a last-ditch effort to continue the metal range, but it failed against the competition from the imported Matchbox cars, which were less expensive and of better quality. The knowledgeable collector will seek out the two-tone models in this series because they were the only postwar Tootsietoys that were well-painted.

In the six-inch series the 1959 Chevrolet semi-truck and the Chrysler 300 are rarest. Coming at the end of a production cycle, they were produced in small numbers. Other rare items in this line are the Kaiser, the 1948 Buick Wagon and the 1950 Chrysler with its separately cast windshield. The most frequently found cars in the six-inch series today are the

**1947 STUDEBAKER CHAM-
PION COUPE, FIVE-WINDOW.
THE RAREST THREE-INCH.**

**1950 TWIN COACH BUS. A
VERY RARE THREE-INCH.**

1947 JEEPSTER, THREE-INCH.

**1954 NASH METROPOLITAN
CONVERTIBLE, THREE
INCHES.**

**1955 FORD CUSTOMLINE V-8
TWO-DOOR SEDAN, THREE
INCHES.**

four 1936 Jumbo/Torpedo series models that the firm continued to produce until 1950: the Auburn Roadster, Pierce-Arrow Coupe, Hupmobile Sedan and International Pickup Truck. The 1959 Ford Wagon and 1959 Oldsmobile are also easy to find. The Jeep CJ3 and CJ5 came in many variations, as the windshield was cast either separately or integrally with the body and either upright or folded down; the Jeeps were also cast with and without a plow and in both army and civilian versions. The most collectible of the six-inchers are the two-tone models with tin chassis, followed by the two-tone types without chassis. The rarest in any range are the trailers, but they are also the least valuable, as trailers in any series are not in great demand. The six-inch model with the lowest production run, and thus the rarest today, is the restaurant trailer. The house trailer was produced in the greatest numbers and is the most readily found.

The small series of nine-inch cars was made for only a few years in the United States and never gained much popularity, proving as before that Tootsietoys were most successful in the low-priced field. All nine-inch models have a heavy diecast Zamak chassis, interior detail, and good paint. The 1955 Pontiac has a two-piece tailgate that opens, and the Mercedes 300 SL has two gull-wing doors that open. Both are currently produced in Mexico. The other nine-incher is the Austin-Healey 100-6.

In hopes of moving into the market for more expensive toys, Tootsietoy made arrangements in 1960 with the British firm of Lone Star to manufacture a series of American cars to compete directly with the popular Dinky Toys and Corgi Toys. These cars, known as Tootsietoy Classics, had coil spring suspension, windows, plated bumpers and grilles, and demountable tires on plated metal hubs. In 1961 detailed interiors were added. The models made by Lone Star for sale in the United States were marked TOOTSIETOY MADE IN ENGLAND; those sold in Canada and the rest of the world were marked LONE STAR MADE IN ENGLAND. The Lone Star models were marketed by Tootsietoy only in 1960 and 1961 and were the best-quality Tootsietoys ever offered. After 1961 Lone Star continued to produce these cars under their own name, and they were sold in America until 1968, but through a different distributor and at a much-reduced volume. The quality of these models was poorer, but the series was expanded to include a Rolls-Royce Silver Cloud, Citroën DS19 and 1960 Chevrolet El Camino pickup truck, plus specialized issues of the earlier cars: a Dodge Polara police car, Corvair fire chief's car and army staff car, and Rambler civilian and army ambulances. Some of the Lone Star versions were sold in Canada but not in the United States.

In 1960 the Tootsietoy firm itself produced a series of antique cars which were included in the Tootsietoy Classic line and sold at the same price as the imported Lone Star cars: fifty-nine cents. These old-timers remained in production until 1965. All of the antique models were made with metal wheels in 1960 and plastic wheels from then on. The Mack Truck included a plastic rear body; the Model T and Model A Fords, Stutz Bearcat, Cadillac and Stanley Steamer had completely diecast bodies. All models of the Classic series are equally rare today.

The Tootsietoy firm has always been successful in producing low-cost items. In 1946 their products sold for ten, fifteen and nineteen cents for the three-, four- and six-inch series. With the gradual increase in the cost of living, the prices reached twenty-nine, thirty-nine and fifty-nine cents by 1960. This was more than the cost of a Matchbox car at that time, and a product was needed to compete in the lower-priced market. So the Jam-Pac toys were introduced, very simple one-inch castings that were usually sold in sets of ten for a dollar, or for ten cents apiece. The firm also went into the production of large vinyl toys, which do not concern us here. Present-day Tootsietoys include numerous motor vehicles, but they are more than ever "toys for doodling, not models for collecting."

Most of the Tootsietoy dies from the late fifties are still being used for production in Mexico, where the toys are made exclusively for the Mexican market. They are still marked TOOTSIETOY MADE IN U.S.A. and can be told from the earlier U.S. issues by their wheels. Mexi-

1955 CHEVROLET BEL AIR SIX-CYLINDER FOUR-DOOR SEDAN, THREE INCHES.

1957 FORD F100 STYLESIDE PICKUP, WITH AND WITHOUT REAR WINDOW, THREE-INCH.

1954 AMERICAN LA FRANCE PUMPER, THREE-INCH.

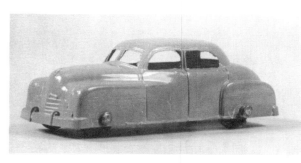

1950 PLYMOUTH SPECIAL DELUXE FOUR-DOOR SEDAN, THREE-INCH.

1952 FORD MAINLINE FOUR-DOOR SEDAN, THREE-INCH.

can Tootsietoys have a smooth rubber type of wheel with a barely visible white film. The most collectible versions are those with Spanish-language decals for Mexican companies, such as the PeMex Oil Tanker and the Moving Van.

Copies of many prewar Tootsietoys have been produced recently by the small American firm of Accucast. The Accucast models are slightly heavier than the original Tootsietoys, and the unpainted metal parts have a higher shine. The easiest to detect are the 230 series of three-inch models such as the 1938 Ford Wagon, because of their much greater weight. In addition, Accucast has produced Tootsietoy models that were never marketed but were only in the planning stage. These include the 1928 Model A Ford Roadster and Five Window Coupe. Accucast has also made a 'super series' of the 1926 G.M. line with a separate chassis, separate grille with headlights, and demountable tires. The Tootsietoy G.M. series lacked these features, and as a result the Accucast copies look more realistic than the originals. A problem for the collector is that it is hard to tell some Accucast copies from the originals, especially in that some original Tootsietoys were never marked with their manufacturer's name, while some Accucast copies are so marked. Other copies of various prewar Tootsietoys are also on the market.

This concludes our look at the Tootsietoy models. We hope this book will afford collectors a more thorough knowledge of Tootsietoys and their history, and will at least stimulate a nostalgic interest among non-collectors—and perhaps even inspire them to join our ranks. Happy hobbying to you all!

1957 JAGUAR TYPE D,
THREE-INCH.

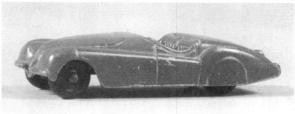

1954 JAGUAR XK120 ROAD-
STER, THREE INCHES.

1960 FORD COUNTRY SEDAN
STATION WAGON, THREE-
INCH.

1931 FORD B HOT ROD.
MADE IN 1960; THREE
INCHES.

1947 OFFENHAUSER HILL
CLIMBER, THREE-INCH.

1949 FORD CUSTOM FOUR-
DOOR SEDAN, AND 1949
FORD CUSTOM CON-
VERTIBLE. BOTH ARE THREE
INCHES.

1949 FORD F1 PICKUP,
THREE-INCH.

1950 CHEVROLET FLEETLINE
DELUXE TWO-DOOR SEDAN
(FASTBACK), THREE INCHES.

1956 TRIUMPH TR3 ROAD-
STER, THREE-INCH.

1956 FORD C600 OIL TANK-
ER, THREE INCHES.

1957 FORD FAIRLANE 500
CONVERTIBLE, THREE-INCH.

1957 PLYMOUTH BELVEDERE
TWO-DOOR HARDTOP,
THREE INCHES.

1960 FORD FALCON TWO-
DOOR SEDAN, THREE-INCH.

1960 STUDEBAKER LARK
CUSTOM CONVERTIBLE,
THREE-INCH.

1949 OLDSMOBILE 88 CON-
VERTIBLE, FOUR-INCH.

1949 MERCURY FIRE CHIEF
AND CIVILIAN FOUR-DOOR
SEDANS, FOUR-INCH.

1941 CHRYSLER WINDSOR
CONVERTIBLE. POSTWAR IS-
SUE, FOUR INCHES.

1941 INTERNATIONAL K1
PANEL. FOUR-INCH POST-
WAR.

1955 OLDSMOBILE 98 HOLI-
DAY TWO-DOOR HARDTOP.
ALSO AVAILABLE IN ARMY
VERSION, FOUR INCHES.

1954-55 CORVETTE ROAD-
STER, FOUR INCHES.

1959 PONTIAC STAR CHIEF FOUR-DOOR SEDAN, FOUR-INCH.

1960 CHRYSLER WINDSOR CONVERTIBLE, FOUR-INCH.

1969 FORD LTD TWO-DOOR HARDTOP, FOUR INCHES. ALL TOOTSIETOYS MADE AFTER THIS ONE ARE PLASTIC.

1938 BUICK Y EXPERIMENTAL ROADSTER, POSTWAR ISSUE, FOUR INCHES.

1941 WHITE ARMY HALF TRACK. POSTWAR ISSUE, FOUR INCHES.

1947 BUICK SPECIAL FAST-
BACK. SOMETIMES CALLED
CHEVROLET FLEETMASTER,
FOUR INCHES.

1949 FORD F6 OIL TANKER,
FOUR-INCH.

1949 FORD F6 STAKE TRUCK,
FOUR-INCH.

1950 PONTIAC CHIEFTAIN
DELUXE COUPE SEDAN,
FOUR INCHES. ALSO AVAIL-
ABLE AS FIRE CHIEF.

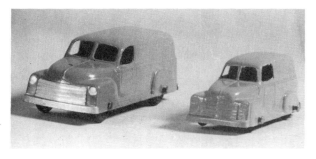

1950 CHEVROLET DELUXE
PANEL, FOUR-INCH AND
THREE-INCH. FOUR-INCH AL-
SO AVAILABLE AS CIVILIAN
OR ARMY AMBULANCE.

1950 DODGE PICKUP, FOUR-INCH.

1950 JEEP CJ3 ARMY, FOUR-INCH AND THREE-INCH. ALSO AVAILABLE AS CIVILIAN IN BOTH SIZES.

1952 MERCURY CUSTOM FOUR-DOOR SEDAN, FOUR INCHES.

NO. 1040 HOOK AND LADDER TRUCK (POSTWAR), FOUR INCHES.

NO. 1041 HOSE CAR (POSTWAR), FOUR INCHES.

1954 FORD RANCH WAGON, FOUR AND THREE INCHES.

1955 THUNDERBIRD COUPE, FOUR AND THREE INCHES.

1956 CHEVROLET CAMEO PICKUP, FOUR INCHES.

1960 RAMBLER SUPER CROSS-COUNTRY SIX-CYLINDER WAGON, FOUR INCHES.

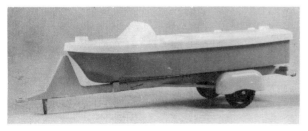

BOAT TRAILER, FOUR INCHES. SOLD ONLY IN SETS.

UNKNOWN MAKE—COULD
BE A FOUR-INCH HUDSON
OR INTERNATIONAL METRO.
MADE IN 1947.

ASSORTED TRAILERS FOR
FOUR- AND SIX-INCH CARS.

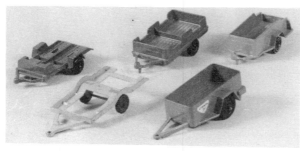

1959 CHEVROLET SEMI WITH
GOOSENECK TRAILER. A
VERY RARE SIX-INCH.

1947 KAISER SEDAN, SIX-
INCH.

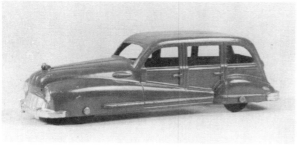

1948 BUICK SUPER ESTATE
WAGON. THE RAREST SIX-
INCH.

1950 CHRYSLER WINDSOR
CONVERTIBLE, SIX-INCH
(WINDSHIELD RARELY COM-
PLETE).

1959 OLDSMOBILE DYNAMIC
88 CONVERTIBLE, SIX
INCHES.

1960 JEEP CJ5, SIX-INCH.
ALSO AVAILABLE IN ARMY
AND SNOWPLOW VERSIONS.

TIN CHASSIS FOR CADILLAC,
SIMILAR TO THOSE USED
ON MOST SIX-INCH MODELS
IN 1954-56.

1940 FORD V-8 HOT ROD.
MADE IN 1960, SIX INCHES.

1940 FORD SPECIAL DELUXE CONVERTIBLE. MADE IN 1960, SIX INCHES.

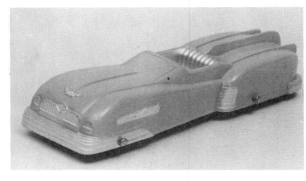

1942 CHRYSLER THUNDER-BOLT EXPERIMENTAL ROAD-STER, SIX-INCH POSTWAR IS-SUE.

1947 MACK L-LINE DUMP, SIX-INCH.

1947 MACK L-LINE TOW, SIX-INCH.

1947 MACK L-LINE WITH NEWER VAN TRAILER, SIX-INCH.

1947 MACK L-LINE WITH OLD-
ER VAN TRAILER (NO REAR
DOORS), SIX-INCH.

1947 MACK L-LINE FIRE
PUMPER, SIX-INCH.

1947 MACK L-LINE STAKE,
CLOSED-SIDE, SIX INCHES.

1947 MACK L-LINE WITH
STAKE TRAILER, SIX-INCH.

1947 MACK L-LINE WITH FIRE
TRAILER. ONLY L-LINE TRAIL-
ER WITH SINGLE REAR
TIRES. SIX INCHES.

1946 INTERNATIONAL K11
OIL TANKER, STANDARD
AND SINCLAIR. WAS ALSO
AVAILABLE AS SHELL AND
TEXACO, SIX-INCHES.

1948 GMC 3751 GREYHOUND
BUS, SIX-INCH.

1948 CADILLAC 60 SPECIAL
FOUR-DOOR SEDAN, SIX-
INCH.

1949 FORD F6 OIL TANKER,
SHELL. ALSO AVAILABLE AS
TEXACO, STANDARD OR SIN-
CLAIR, SIX-INCH.

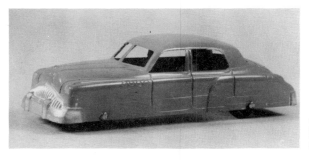

1949 BUICK ROADMASTER
FOUR-DOOR SEDAN. A RARE
SIX-INCH MODEL.

1951 BUICK LE SABRE EX-PERIMENTAL ROADSTER, SIX-INCH.

1952 LINCOLN CAPRI TWO-DOOR HARDTOP, SIX INCHES.

1953 CHRYSLER NEW YORK-ER FOUR-DOOR SEDAN, SIX-INCH.

1954 BUICK SPECIAL EXPERI-MENTAL COUPE, SIX INCHES.

1954 CADILLAC 62 FOUR-DOOR SEDAN, SIX INCHES.

1954 MG TF SIX- AND THREE-
INCH ROADSTERS. SIX-INCH
CAME WITH AND WITHOUT
PLASTIC MAN.

1954 BUICK CENTURY ES-
TATE WAGON, SIX INCHES.

1955 MACK B-LINE WITH
STAKE TRAILER (CLOSED
VERSION), SIX INCHES.

1955 MACK B-LINE CEMENT
MIXER, SIX INCHES.

1955 INTERNATIONAL RC180
WITH GRAIN TRAILER, SIX
INCHES.

1955 INTERNATIONAL RC180 WITH TRANSPORT TRAILER, SIX INCHES.

1955 FORD F600 STAKE TRUCK. TIN COVER IS VERY RARE, SIX INCHES.

1956 PORSCHE SPYDER ROADSTER, SIX INCHES.

1956 LANCIA, SIX INCHES.

1956 FERRARI, SIX INCHES.

1956 MERCEDES 190SL
COUPE, SIX INCHES.

1956 AUSTIN-HEALEY 100-6
FOUR-PASSENGER ROAD-
STER, SIX INCHES.

1956 PACKARD PATRICIAN
FOUR-DOOR SEDAN, SIX
INCHES.

1956 CATERPILLAR SCRAPER,
SIX INCHES.

1956 CATERPILLAR DOZER.
AVAILABLE WITH OR WITH-
OUT BLADE, SIX-INCH.

**1956 JAGUAR XK140 COUPE,
SIX-INCH.**

**1956 DODGE D100 PANEL,
SIX INCHES.**

**1957 GMC GREYHOUND
SCENICRUISER BUS, SIX-
INCH.**

**1959 FORD COUNTRY SEDAN
STATION WAGON, SIX-INCH.**

**1960 INTERNATIONAL
METRO VAN. RARE SIX-INCH.**

1960 EL CAMINO WITH CAMP-
ER AND BOAT. ALSO MADE
AS JUST A PICKUP, SIX IN-
CHES.

1960 VOLKSWAGEN 113
BUGS, SIX AND THREE
INCHES.

1962 FORD ECONOLINE
PICKUP, SIX INCHES.

1962 FORD COUNTRY SEDAN
STATION WAGON, SIX
INCHES.

1962 FORD C600, SIX
INCHES.

HORSE TRAILER, SIX INCHES. RARE. SOLD ONLY IN SETS WITH A CAR.

BOAT TRAILER, SIX INCHES. SOLD ONLY IN SETS.

RESTAURANT TRAILER, SIX INCHES. THE RAREST TRAILER.

HOUSE TRAILER, SIX INCHES. VERY COMMON.

HO SERIES: 1960 CADILLAC, 1960 RAMBLER, 1960 FORD CONVERTIBLE, INTERNATIONAL FARM TRACTOR, AND 1960 FORD. THESE MODELS ARE ABOUT THE SIZE OF A MATCHBOX. IN SERIES BUT NOT PICTURED ARE A SCHOOL BUS AND A METRO VAN.

ENGLISH-MADE 1960 CADILLAC SERIES 62 FOUR-DOOR HARDTOP, FOUR-WINDOW MODEL, FOUR INCHES.

ENGLISH-MADE 1960 FORD GALAXIE 500 SUNLINER CONVERTIBLE, FOUR INCHES.

ENGLISH-MADE 1960 RAMBLER SUPER SIX CROSS-COUNTRY WAGON, FOUR INCHES.

1921 MACK AC DUMP WITH BODY MISSING, ISSUED IN 1960.

1906 CADILLAC COUPE. IN
THE FOUR-INCH ANTIQUE
SERIES, MADE IN 1960.

1907 STANLEY STEAMER
RUNABOUT. IN THE FOUR-
INCH ANTIQUE SERIES,
MADE IN 1960.

1912 FORD MODEL T TOUR-
ING CAR. IN THE 1960 AN-
TIQUE SERIES, FOUR
INCHES.

1929 FORD MODEL A COUPE,
ISSUED IN THE 1960 FOUR-
INCH ANTIQUE SERIES.

1919 STUTZ BEARCAT. FROM
THE FOUR-INCH ANTIQUE
SERIES MADE IN 1960.

MEXICAN TOOTSIE (STILL AVAILABLE); 1955 INTERNATIONAL RC180 SEMI WITH VAN TRAILER. SIX INCHES, OTHER DECALS AVAILABLE.

MEXICAN TOOTSIE (STILL AVAILABLE); 1955 INTERNATIONAL RC180 PEMEX OIL TANKER, SIX INCHES.

ACCUCAST 1919 FORD MODEL T FIRE TRUCK.

ACCUCAST SUPER SERIES 1926 CHEVROLET ROADSTER. BASED ON GM 1926 SERIES WITH HEADLIGHTS, BUMPER, SEPARATE GRILLE AND DEMOUNTABLE RIMS ADDED.

ACCUCAST 001Y 1926 DELIVERY VAN, EMIL KRAUS.

1926 CHEVROLET DELIVERY
VAN (ESKIMO PIE) ISSUED
BY ACCUCAST.

1926 CHEVROLET DELIVERY
TRUCK (WRIGLEY'S) ISSUED
BY ACCUCAST. DIFFERENT
FEATURES FROM THE ORIG-
INAL TOOTSIETOY INCLUDE
SEPARATE GRILLE WITH
HEADLIGHTS AND DE-
MOUNTABLE TIRES.

ACCUCAST 1928 FORD
MODEL A FIVE-WINDOW
COUPE. THE TOOTSIETOY
WAS A THREE-WINDOW.

1928 FORD MODEL A ROAD-
STER, ISSUED BY AC-
CUCAST.

TOOTSIETOY FLYER.

PENNSYLVANIA PASSENGER
TRAIN (POSTWAR).

APPENDIX

The following is a list of Tootsietoys not pictured in the text.

CATALOGUE NUMBER	DESCRIPTION	FIRST ISSUE	SIZE	MM
10	Auto and Garage Set	ca 1925		
11	Train and Station Set	ca 1925		
104	Mack Insurance Patrol (1930 Mack AC)	1932	1/87	59
107	High Wing Monoplane	1932		
114	Ford Convertible Coupe (1934 Ford V-8)	1935	3 inch	76
115	Ford Convertible Sedan (1934 Ford V-8)	1935	3 inch	76

NOTE: *Some 100-121 numbers were used for dollhouse furniture in the twenties.*

CATALOGUE NUMBER	DESCRIPTION	FIRST ISSUE	SIZE	MM
135	5¢ Boat Assortment	ca 1940		
160	The World Flyers	1925		
170	Interchangeable Truck Set (1921 Mack AC)	1925	1/72	
179	Mosquito Fleet	ca 1940		
180	Roamer Set	1938	1/43	
184	Fire Department Set	ca 1940		
185	Fire Department Set	1927		
189	Air Raiders Set	ca 1940		
197	Battery Set	1933		
199	Playtime Set	ca 1940		
203	Water Pistol	ca 1925		
260	Yellow Cab (pilot model)	1941		
261	Checker Cab (pilot model)	1941		
262	Fire Engine (pilot model)	1941		
263	Hook and Ladder Truck (pilot model)	1941		
411	Fire Department Set	1938		
511	Graham 5-wheel Roadster (1932 Graham Blue Streak 8)	1933	1/43	
513	Graham 5-wheel Sedan (1932 Graham Blue Streak 8)	1933	1/43	
514	Graham 5-wheel Convertible Coupe (1932 Blue Streak 8)	1933	1/43	
515	Graham 5-wheel Convertible Sedan (1932 Blue Streak 8)	1933	1/43	
525	Rol-Ezy Assortment	ca 1940		
550	Fire Department Assortment	ca 1940		
575	Aeroplane Assortment	ca 1940		
612	Graham 6-wheel Coupe (1932 Blue Streak 8)	1933	1/43	
614	Graham 6-wheel Convertible Coupe (1932 Blue Streak 8)	1933	1/43	
615	Graham 6-wheel Convertible Sedan (1932 Blue Streak 8)	1933	1/43	
616	Graham 6-wheel Town Car (Blue Streak 8)	1933	1/43	
650	Army Set	ca 1940		
714	LaSalle Convertible Coupe (1935 LaSalle V-8)	1935	1/43	108
715	LaSalle Convertible Sedan (1935 LaSalle V-8)	1935	1/43	108
718	Waco Navy Bomber	1937		
719	Crusader Plane	1937		
720	Fly-n-Gyro	1938		
721	Curtis P-40 Pursuit Plane	1941		
722	Transport Plane	1941		95
750	Jumbo Set	1941		
1005	Oil Truck Assortment	ca 1941		
1025	Torpedo Assortment	ca 1940		
1050	Fire Department Assortment	ca 1940		
1075	Aeroplane Assortment	ca 1940		
1076	Santa Fe Locomotive	1939		

CATALOGUE NUMBER	DESCRIPTION	FIRST ISSUE	SIZE	MM
1081	10ᶜ Boat Assortment	ca 1940		
1085	Freight Assortment	ca 1940		
1404	Land Defense Set	ca 1940		
1407	Air Defense Set	ca 1940		
1408	Naval Defense Set	ca 1940		
4314	Police Whistle	ca 1925		
4341	Telephone	ca 1925		
4397	Train	ca 1921		
4400	Folding Go-Cart	ca 1921		
4402	Desk (for dollhouse)	ca 1925		
4446	Candleholder	ca 1925		
4465	Clermont	ca 1921		
4491	Bleriot Aeroplane (small)	1910		
4521	Candelabra	ca 1925		
4522	Candelabra	ca 1925		
4524	Candelabra	ca 1925		
4595	Thunderer Whistle	ca 1925		
4601	Horse on Wheels	ca 1925		
4602	Dog on Wheels	ca 1925		
4603	Lion on Wheels	ca 1925		
4620	Locomotive	ca 1925		
4621	Tender	ca 1925		
4623	Pullman Coach	ca 1925		
4624	Gondola Car	ca 1925		
4625	Military Assortment	ca 1940		
4650	Biplane	1926		80
4656	Buick Coupe (see also 101)	1931		58
4657	Buick Sedan (see also 103)	1931		58
4662	Mortar	1931		
5000	Motor Set	ca 1940		
5041	Air Mail Set	1931		
5050	Playtime Toys Set	ca 1940		
5071	Field Battery Set	1931		
5081	Speedway Set	1932		
5091	Funnies Set	1932		
5100	Airport Set	1930		
5100	Playtime Set	ca 1940		
5150	Motor Set	1940		
5210	Truck Set (1936-38) or Commercial Set (1939-41)	ca 1941		
5220	Army Set	ca 1941		
5300	Tootsietoy Motors Set	1933		
5310	Truck Set	1933		
5350	Taxicab Set	1933		
5360	Bild-a-Car Set	1933		
5550	Freight Set	ca 1940		
5600	Freight Set	ca 1940		
5700	Navy Fleet	ca 1940		
5750	Navy Set	ca 1940		
5850	Passenger Limited Set	ca 1940		
5851	Santa Fe Set	ca 1940		
5900	Convoy Set	ca 1940		
6001	Buick Roadster (1926 Buick Series 50)	1927	1/43	
6002	Buick Coupe (1926 Buick Series 50)	1927	1/43	
6004	Buick Sedan (1926 Buick Series 50)	1927	1/43	
6005	Buick Touring Car (1926 Buick Series 50)	1927	1/43	
6006	Buick Delivery Truck (1926 Buick Series 50)	1927	1/43	
6100	Aeroplane Set	1941		
6101	Cadillac Roadster (1926 Cadillac Standard V-8)	1927	1/43	
6103	Cadillac Brougham (1926 Cadillac Standard V-8)	1927	1/43	
6105	Cadillac Touring Car (Cadillac Standard V-8)	1927	1/43	

CATALOGUE NUMBER	DESCRIPTION	FIRST ISSUE	SIZE	MM
6106	Cadillac Delivery Truck (Cadillac Standard V-8)	1927	1/43	
6150	Aeroplane Set	ca 1940	1/43	
6202	Chevrolet Coupe (1926 Chevrolet)	1927	1/43	
6203	Chevrolet Brougham (1926 Chevrolet)	1927	1/43	
6204	Chevrolet Sedan (1926 Chevrolet)	1927	1/43	
6205	Chevrolet Touring Car (1926 Chevrolet)	1927	1/43	
6206	Chevrolet Delivery Truck (1926 Chevrolet)	1927	1/43	
6301	Oldsmobile Roadster (1926 Oldsmobile Standard 6)	1927	1/43	
6302	Oldsmobile Coupe (1926 Oldsmobile Standard 6)	1927	1/43	
6303	Oldsmobile Brougham (1926 Oldsmobile Standard 6)	1927	1/43	
6304	Oldsmobile Sedan (1926 Oldsmobile Standard 6)	1927	1/43	
6305	Oldsmobile Touring Car (Oldsmobile Standard 6)	1927	1/43	

6-INCH MODELS

1940 International K5 Truck (Semi Grain Trailer, Semi Van)
1947 Mack L-Line Truck (Tow, Semi Closed Stake, Semi Van, Semi Moving Van, Semi Oil [2 types], Semi Grain, Semi Log, Semi Pipe, Dump)
1955 Chrysler 300 2-door Hardtop
1955 Mack B Line (Semi Open Stake, Semi Oil, Semi Hook-n-ladder, Semi Moving Van, Semi Pipe, Semi Log)
1955 International RC180 (Semi Oil, Semi Gooseneck, Semi Moving Van, Semi Boat Transport)
1956 Ford Farm Tractor with attachments: harrow, plow, manure spreader

POSTWAR TOOTSIETOY SOLD ONLY IN SETS WITH A CAR

6-inch   U-Haul Trailer, 2 types
4-inch   Cargo Trailer
4-inch   Race Car Trailer

9-INCH 1/25 METAL TOOTSIETOY

1955 Pontiac Safari Wagon 2-door
1955 Mercedes 300 SL Gullwing Coupe
1955 Austin Healey 100-6 4-passenger

4-INCH IMPORTED TOOTSIETOY

1960 Chevrolet Corvair 4-door Sedan

HO SERIES

School Bus
Metro Van

UNNUMBERED MODELS

Farm Box Trailer	1928		
Road Scraper-Hayrake Trailer	1928		
Aero-Dawn Seaplane	1928 or later		
Wings Seaplane	1929 or later		
Army Gun Tractor	1931		
GM Series no-name Coupe (1926 Oakland)	1933	1/43	
GM Series no-name Delivery Truck (1926 Oakland)	1933	1/43	
Graham 4-wheel Roadster (1932 Graham Blue Streak)	1933	1/43	
Graham 4-wheel Coupe (1932 Graham Blue Streak)	1933	1/43	
Graham 4-wheel Sedan (1932 Graham Blue Streak)	1933	1/43	
Single Engine Transport	1942?		

Not included are paint variations such as the Graham Sedan Taxi, Graham Army Ambulance, Army Caterpillar Tractor, the numbered Racers from the Speedway Set and other minor variations. Also not included are numerous sets whose numbers we have not been able to ascertain.

Bibliography

Anderson, Arthur E. "The Tootsietoy Era." *Miniature Auto*, Vol. II, No. 12, pp. 376-78; and Vol. III, No. 1, pp. 18-20; plus follow-up letter, Vol. III, No. 5, p. 158.

Borgeson, Griffith. *The Golden Age of the American Racing Car*. New York: Bonanza Books, 1966.

The B. P. Book of World Land Speed Records. London: Herbert Jenkins Ltd., 1963.

Burness, Tad. *American Car Spotter's Guide 1920-1939*. Osceola, Wisconsin: Motorbooks International, 1975.

————. *American Car Spotter's Guide 1940-1965*. Osceola, Wisconsin: Motorbooks International, 1973.

Cutter, Robert, and Bob Fendell. *Encyclopedia of Auto Racing Greats*. Englewood Cliffs, New Jersey: Prentice-Hall, 1973.

Encyclopedia of Aviation. New York: Charles Scribner's & Sons, 1977.

Force, Ed. "Some Random Shots at Tootsietoys." *C.A.R.S.* (La Mirada, California, Collectors' Automotive Replica Society), Vol. IV, No. 3, pp. 3-5.

————. "Those Wonderful Old Tootsietoys." *C.A.R.S.* (La Mirada, California, Collectors' Automotive Replica Society), Vol. II, No. 4, pp. 1-4.

Gibson, Cecil. *Commercial Vehicles*. London: Thomas Nelson & Sons Ltd., 1970.

————. *A History of British Dinky Toys 1934-1964*. Windsor, England: Mikansue, 1976.

————. *Veteran and Vintage Cars*. London: Thomas Nelson & Sons Ltd., 1970.

Greilsamer, Jacques, and Bertrand Azema. *Catalogue Mondiale des Modèles Reduits Automobiles*. Lausanne, Switzerland: Edita, 1967.

Hertz, Louis H. *The Complete Book of Building and Collecting Model Automobiles*. New York: Crown Publishers, 1970.

Jewell, F. Brian. *Model Car Collecting*. London: Temple Press, 1963.

Lee, C.B.C. "Early Tootsietoy Aircraft." *Modellers' World*, Vol. III, No. 2, pp. 6-8.

————. "A History of Pre-War Automotive Tootsietoys." *Model Cars*, Vol. VIII, Nos. 1-9; reprinted in *The Antique Toy World*, Vol. II, Nos. 5-12.

————. "Early Tootsie Toys." *Model Car Collector*, Issue No. 2, pp. 15-17; and Issue No. 3, pp. 9-15.

————. "New Pieces in the Tootsie Puzzle." *C.A.R.S.* (Millbrae, California, Collectors' Automotive Replica Society), Vol. VI, No. 1, pp. 6-7.

————. "Some Other Dolomites." *C.A.R.S.* (San Carlos, California, Collectors' Automotive Replica Society), Vol. III, No. 2, pp. 7-8.

————. "Special Department Store Tootsietoy Trucks." *C.A.R.S.* (San Carlos, California, Collectors' Automotive Replica Society), Vol. IV, No. 3, p. 9.

————. "Store Federals." *The Antique Toy World*, Vol. IV, No. 2, pp. 6-9.

————. "Tootsietoy Postscript." *Miniature Auto*, Vol. IV, No. 3, p. 17.

————. "When Tootsietoy Set the Pace." *Miniature Auto*, Vol. IV, No. 2, pp. 10-12.

Lee, Randy. "The Roamer Trailer." *Model Car Journal*, Vol. V, No. 1, p. 14.

Norboru Nakajima. *Minicar*. Hoikusha Color Books, No. 127.

Seeley, Clinton B. "Collectors' Pieces." *Miniature Auto*, Vol. III, No. 5, p. 156.

————. "Quand les Tootsietoys coutaient 10 cents!" *Modélism*, No. 77, pp. 84-85.

Williams, Guy R. *The World of Model Cars*. London: André Deutsch, 1976.

Automotive library additions

American Car Spotter's Guide 1940-1965. Covers 66 makes—almost 3,000 illustrations. 358 pages, softbound.

American Car Spotter's Guide 1966-1980. Giant pictorial source with over 3,600 illustrations. 432 pages, softbound.

American Truck Spotter's Guide 1920-1970. 170 makes are covered with over 2,000 illustrations. Softbound, 330 pages.

The Big "Little GTO" Book. All of these Great Ones by Pontiac are covered—1965-1974. Over 150 great photos, 235 pages. Large format, softbound.

Chevy Super Sports 1961-1976. Exciting story of these hot cars with complete specs and data. 176 pages, 234 illustrations, softbound. Large format.

Son of Muscle Car Mania. 176 pages of more great ads from the 1962-1974 muscle car era. All U.S. makes represented. Softbound, 250 illustrations.

Fearsome Fords 1959-1973. Over 250 photos of these great cars accompany 182 pages of interesting information. Softbound, large format.

Mighty Mopars. The story of these great cars is told, 1960–1974. Includes over 175 great illustrations, softbound.

Corgi Toys: The Ones With Windows. All about these detailed British diecasts; over 350 photos—nearly 400 models. 117 pages, softbound.

Motoring Mascots of the World. Lavish collection of hood mascots accompanied by informative text. 196 pages, 802 illustrations.

Shelby's Wildlife: The Cobras and Mustangs. Complete, exciting story of the 260, 289, 427 and Daytona Cobras plus Shelby Mustangs. 224 pages, nearly 200 photos.

Classic Motorbooks Chevy El Camino 1959-1982 Photofacts. 80 pages packed full of info on these car/trucks. Softbound, about 200 photos.

Classic Motorbooks Chrysler 300 1955-1961 Photofacts. Over 125 photos accompany lots of info on these cars. Softbound, 80 pages.

Classic Motorbooks Pontiac Trans Am 1969-1973 Photofacts. Over 125 great photos help tell the story. 80 pages, softbound.

Bob Bondurant on High Performance Driving. World-famous instructor teaches secrets to fast, safe driving. Over 100 illustrations, 144 pages, softbound.

Classic Motorbooks Ford Retractable 1957-1959 Photofacts. Nearly 200 photos help tell this unique story. Softbound, 80 pages.

The Art and Science of Grand Prix Driving. Complete analysis and discussion by World Champion Niki Lauda. Over 150 photos, 23 in color, 245 pages.

Illustrated Austin-Healey Buyer's Guide. The 100 through the 300 through the Jensen-Healey are covered with over 125 great illustrations. Softbound, 136 pages.

How To Restore Your Collector Car. Covers all the major restoration processes in an easy to understand, easy to use format. More than 300 illustrations. Softbound, 320 pages.

Harley-Davidson Motor Company: An Official Eighty-Year History. More than 250 photos plus 8 pages of color tell the complete story of the company 1903–1983. 288 pages.

Motorbooks International
Publishers & Wholesalers Inc.
Osceola, Wisconsin 54020, USA